Pushing the Edge

Thought, Possibility, and Action

QUESTIONS AND INSIGHTS FROM EVERYDAY LIFE

by Glenn E. Mangurian

FRONTIERWORKS PUBLISHING

Pushing the Edge: Thought, Possibility, and Action
Questions and Insights from Everyday Life

To Gail

My Wife, My Love, and the Angel Who Guides My Life

Acknowledgments

This book is a snapshot from a lifetime of experiences, observations, and learnings. All my interactions have had some role in contributing to these insights.

SANDRA MANGURIAN for your encouragement and editorial experience on the publishing journey

My children, LAURA and MARK, for making me proud every day

RON DONOVAN and STEVE STANTON for your advice on how to self-publish a book

GERRY LOEV for being my mentor and teaching me how to think

My CSC INDEX COLLEAGUES for 21 years of partnership and learning

My CLIENTS for your willingness to accept me pushing the edge of your thinking

MARY FORD for your support as a columnist in the *Hingham Journal*

BALAJI KRISHRAHURTHY for the example you set through your provocative *Food for Thought* essays

MARINA DONNELLY for your critical eyes and thoughtful editing

BRIDGET SMITH for your insight and creativity on book and cover design

Contents

Introduction

My 40-year career advising professionals in North America and Europe has encompassed a broad range of sectors of the economic spectrum—I've coached private and public leaders in education, healthcare, and justice . My focus has been helping my clients to realize—to imagine and achieve—new levels of performance. For many of them, ambitious performance seemed out of reach. They doubted their organization's ability to embrace, adapt to, and execute new ways of operating.

My own belief in ambitious possibilities was tested in 2001 after I suffered a freak injury to my spinal cord, which rendered my lower body paralyzed. I chronicled my journey of resilience in a *Harvard Business Review* article, "Realizing What You're Made Of."

Shortly after my injury, I started an executive breakfast group of alumni from my alma mater, University of Massachusetts Amherst. I've built a large network over the past 16 years, but the majority of people I interact with only know me operating from a wheelchair—they know little about my career before my injury.

In 2009, I started publishing a monthly essay, "Pushing the Edge." This book is a compendium of some of my most popular essays. The essays are organized into three sections to help you push the edges of thinking, possibility, and action. Each essay begins with a question from everyday life, offers my perspective, and concludes with a set of questions for reflection. We seldom find time to reflect on how our past experiences influence how we see the world today. My objective is not to provide answers to the questions, but to help you gain insight that you'll find relevant and valuable to your life. Enjoy—and have fun pushing the edge.

Pushing the Edge of Thought

We are constantly thinking—exercising our brain—consciously and unconsciously. We think about our past and future opportunities, experiences, and challenges—all while living in the present. We are often in continuous dialogue with an inner voice that is regularly a critic and occasionally a source of encouragement.

All these thoughts are influenced by life experiences, which shape our worldview, values, and belief structures. These experiences form filters through which we see our current circumstances and hear communication from others. Our filters often operate in our subconscious, silently influencing our interpretation of events and steering our actions. Every now and then, though, life's events prompt us to reflect on, question, and even challenge our beliefs and assumptions.

This section poses questions and offers insights about some common aspects of daily life. Consider the questions and reflect on your answers. You might alter your worldview.

Why are we obsessed with asking "why"?

We live in a complex, fast-paced world where events and experiences can be difficult to explain—though that doesn't stop us from trying. We urgently want to know why things happen the way they do, and especially why bad things happen to good people. Why is there undeserved suffering? Theologians, philosophers, and even sociologists have explored our universal need to explain why some people prosper while others suffer. Quite simply, we want answers.

While I'm not a philosopher, I observe the question "why" having five forms or intents:

1. **CURIOSITY WHY.** "Hmm, I'm curious why that happened." We are naturally curious. Curiosity keeps our minds active and allows us to be open to new ideas. Curiosity enables us to see new worlds and possibilities that are hidden beneath the surface of daily life.

2. **SENSE-MAKING WHY.** "What caused this to happen?" We want to make sense of the world around us. We hope the world is rational, so we look for cause-and-effect patterns in life's events. We often ask "why" to better understand the nature of a problem, as well as its possible solution. If we can figure out why something happened, we might be able to prevent it from happening again.

3. **BLAMING WHY.** "I'm really mad that happened. Who is to blame?" Assigning blame is a common way to make sense of things we don't like. We want to know who allowed it to happen and to be assured they will be held accountable.

4. **WALLOWING WHY.** "Why do so many bad things happen to me?" When challenged with adversity, we can easily get stuck asking, "Why me?" But the longer we "wallow in the why," the more likely we are to view the world through the lens of a victim.

3

When that happens, the ongoing questioning "why" can easily stop becoming a search for answers and transform into a statement of powerlessness.

5. **MEANT-TO-BE WHY**. "Are there greater forces at work?" Some things aren't easily explained through logic. Dealing with adversity can prompt us to reflect on our life's purpose. Many discover a deeper meaning in their lives from their spiritual beliefs, a life-meaning that often helps guide them into a purposeful future.

Interestingly, we are not as curious about the "why" when good things happen to us; we seem to take those events for granted. But isn't there just as much to be learned from good outcomes?

Pushing Your Thinking

* When was the last time you obsessed over "why"?
  Were you able to resolve your questions?

* Do you think there is a cause for everything that happens?
  Is it possible that some things "just are," or is everything "meant to be"?

* Why do you think good things happen to you?

Is your word as good as your signature?

Do you remember learning cursive handwriting as a child? Sometime around the second grade, most of us learned how to link our letters with curves. The highlight of these lessons was always learning to write our names in cursive. We were told this was our unique identifier, our signature. I can still remember handing mine out like an autograph, as if I were a famous baseball player.

As we got older, we learned our signature had special meaning when applied to a document—that we were agreeing with its contents or, quite often, agreeing to take responsibility. But in reality, since I was a young man, most of the agreements I've made were in the form of verbal commitments. Even saying something as simple as "I'll be there" carried a lot of weight; people expected me to show up when I said I would. It was in those young adult years of helping friends move and sharing rides when I learned not everyone took their commitments as seriously as I did. Some friends and colleagues would agree to something only "if I have time," while others would fail to deliver on their promise every time, not even offering the courtesy of a warning or explanation.

So how can we tell when someone makes a commitment if the person intends to follow through? Since we can't ask people to swear an oath to fulfill their commitments, my solution is simple: when in doubt, ask the other person to give his or her word. For most of us this is serious stuff. We don't give our word lightly. Our word is more than a commitment for a future action; it's our integrity. Our word creates a bond between people that is hard to take lightly or to break. Our word is a promise with an exclamation point, and breaking our word will likely erode any trust in a relationship.

Children may no longer be learning cursive, e-signatures may have replaced pens, but our word will always be our word. It's our responsibility to give it with integrity.

Pushing Your Thinking

- Is your commitment the same as your word or promise? If not, why not?

- Do you regularly follow through with your commitments? What about your promises? What gets in the way?

- Do you consider others who make a commitment to you as making a promise? Is that how they typically view their commitments?

- When is a commitment not a promise?

- How do we teach children that their word is a promise?

How do you trust those that you trust?

Recently, I taught a module on trust in my graduate leadership course. I asked my adult students the following question: Do you tend to extend trust to others from the start of a relationship, or do they have to earn your trust? The class was split about 50–50. Yet this simple question has profound implications on how we see the world and react to the circumstances we face.

Trust is confident reliance on someone when you are in a position of vulnerability. Trust helps you cope with that vulnerability, reduces conflict, and simplifies difficult decisions. Trust is a curious thing: it can take years to build trust and only seconds to destroy it. We trust (or distrust) people for different reasons, including their expertise, judgment, discretion, emotional support, integrity, and follow-through.

Of course, most of us make trust decisions based on a specific situation, but we tend to lean in one direction or the other. Our tilt is determined by both positive and negative experiences from our past, including our relationships with family and childhood friends, the adversities we have faced, and our story about how we have succeeded.

- **LEAN "A" – ASSUME TRUST.** I give you the benefit of the doubt and consider you trustworthy until you do something that breaks my trust. I assume you have good intentions in our interactions, so I extend my trust to you.

- **LEAN "E" – EARN TRUST.** I am guarded and skeptical of your intentions. I award you my trust only after you've proven yourself.

For the remainder of the course, our class discussions noted the influence of our lean on how we interpret and make decisions around both professional and personal dilemmas.

Here are five questions we ask (mostly subconsciously) when deciding whether to trust another person.

1. What, and how high, are the stakes for me in trusting you?
2. Do you reliably fulfill your promises and commitments?
3. Do I believe you will put yourself at risk for me?
4. Do we have good and open communication?
5. Are our interests aligned?

Remember, it is not just your trust tilt that affects your relationships; others have leans also. Consider interactions between **A** to **A**, **E** to **E**, or **A** to **E** relationships. You can imagine the issues that arise from similar or opposing trust leans.

We need to have trust in people, and we want to trust our institutions. The challenge is to find the right balance between **A** and **E**, between trust and skepticism. Finding this balance is easy for some, but for others it requires real effort.

Pushing Your Thinking

* Which way do you lean? What experiences shaped that lean?
* How has your lean served you, and how has it created problems?
* Whom do you trust and for what reasons?
* Do others trust you? How do you know?
* Do you trust yourself?

What should you ask the person in the mirror?[1]

When was the last time you looked in the mirror and asked yourself some revealing questions?

When we were children, our parents and teachers gave us a great deal of feedback on our behavior and performance. Sometimes we liked it, other times it was hard to hear, but we could be assured they would offer their opinions and advice.

When we entered the workforce, we started to learn more about our strengths and weaknesses from supervisors and mentors, but as we got older and advanced in our careers, these sources of honest and useful feedback dwindled. At a certain point, we felt pretty much on our own.

As adults, we still need guidance and feedback to learn how others experience us. In many cases, our friends and colleagues are reluctant to give us candid feedback, even when asked; being polite often takes precedence over responding with candor.

If we don't develop self-awareness over the years, we can easily lose perspective. Without reliable sources of feedback, we periodically need to step back and reflect on our lives.

Many of us avoid "mirrors" for fear of what our reflection might reveal. It may even take a personal crisis before we examine our beliefs and challenge some long-held assumptions about our lives.

During this time of reflection, it is more important to ask the right questions than to force the answers. The answers will reveal themselves in time.

Pushing Your Thinking

Here are six simple (but maybe profound) questions to ask yourself:

- Do I know who I want to be?
- Am I moving in the right direction?
- Is the way I spend my time consistent with my goals?
- Do my actions reflect who I truly am?
- Am I proud of the contributions that I make?
- Am I content in my life?

The questions may be the same as yesterday, but the answers will likely be different tomorrow. Which questions are most relevant to you right now?

Are you aware of your "buttons"?

No, I don't mean shirt or jacket buttons. You know what I mean—our default reactions in tough moments. We all have them.

Some of our friends, family, and colleagues—and especially our children—know exactly how to push our buttons. When they do, our reactive responses often lead to unproductive behaviors and outcomes. After years of conditioning, though, it's difficult to change these defaults.

Although we may not be able to eliminate these buttons, we can take steps to control our reactions. The first step is to recognize and put a label on the button. Try to dig deep to understand the fundamental worry or insecurity beneath your triggers. Are you sensitive to being dismissed, ignored, or challenged? Second, it is helpful to know when your button typically gets pushed. Does the sight of someone rolling his or her eyes set you off? Is there a question or statement you can't resist reacting to? Third, examine what your default reaction looks like. Are you immediately defensive, angry, or hurt? Do you lash out or withdraw? How does your response make a tough situation worse?

I call one of my buttons the "you're wrong" button. My "you're wrong" button gets pushed after someone reacts to what I intended as an innocent suggestion or casual comment. I don't like being told I'm wrong. I'm okay with a different point of view, but "you're wrong"— that's a different story. "You're wrong" feels so confrontational and sounds so final; it usually shuts down the conversation. My default response is to build a logical argument to defend my position and prove the other person wrong, but this usually makes the situation worse. By digging in my heels, I miss the opportunity to learn what was behind the "you're wrong" comment in the first place. A conversation that started as an innocent statement can easily devolve into an argument that makes all parties uncomfortable.

I recognized my "you're wrong" button quite a while ago. Although I've been unable to eliminate it, I've installed a kind-of circuit breaker, a pause, between the pushing of my button and my response. That pause allows me enough time to consider some overrides:

* Maybe they're right—I might be wrong.
* Maybe it has nothing to do with right or wrong but is merely a difference of opinion.
* Maybe it's not about what I said but how I said it.
* Still, maybe it has nothing to do with me or my assertion but is really about some vulnerability or insecurity in the other person.

I've learned that I can inadvertently push other people's buttons without even knowing it, so I need to be aware of my buttons and conscious of others' as well. Why is life so complicated?

Pushing Your Thinking

* Are you aware of your buttons? Which ones, when pushed, create the strongest impulse to respond?
* How do you respond when your buttons are pushed?
* What can you do to slow your reaction time and create an override?

Next time you get an unanticipated negative response to something you say, consider whether you may have pushed someone else's buttons. Be generous with other people's default reactions—how you respond can escalate or de-escalate the situation.

Whatever happened to make-believe?

Remember the imaginary play of your childhood? Whether we were racing cars through the city or treating a patient as a doctor, we enjoyed bringing toys to a world of make-believe where we channeled our creativity. Over time, our parents, peer pressure, and formal education may conspire to stifle our imaginations. We learned to be realistic, cautious, analytical, and fearful of judgment. Yet as adults, we know that creativity is essential to success in any industry or discipline. Some courses purport to teach creativity, but wouldn't it be more accurate to say they help adults rediscover their natural, childhood abilities?

I recently read an interesting article on unlocking our imaginations.[2] The article was authored by two executives from the design firm IDEO. In the article, they assert that creativity is something you practice, not just a talent you are born with. They argue that without practice, most adults become constrained by four fears that hold back their creativity:

1. **FEAR OF THE FUTURE UNKNOWNS.** We like predictability, and living in a world of messy unknowns can make us feel vulnerable and afraid. We spend precious time and energy trying to prevent future "unknowns" from harming us; but the future is not predictable—we can't see what's coming. Once we reduce or eliminate our fears of the unknown, we can open our minds to discover new areas of exploration.

2. **FEAR OF BEING JUDGED.** In young children, for the most part, the concept of judgment is undeveloped—they take risks and try new skills unconcerned with how others may see them. Yet that awareness increases significantly for teenagers, who care deeply about what others think. It takes only a few years to develop that fear of judgment, but it stays with us throughout our adult lives. What possibilities might we see if we weren't

preoccupied with being judged—what dreams might we create? The fear of being judged can easily prevent us from trying new, uncertain things.

3. **FEAR OF THE FIRST STEP.** Have you ever watched a one-year-old as he or she struggles to gain balance and walk? Toddlers are fearless. Their desire for independence and the freedom to explore vanquishes any fear they have of falling. Yet as adults, we fear challenges as simple as making a phone call to apologize or speaking up in a meeting. Prolonged thinking about doing often prevents us from acting. At IDEO their mantra is "Don't get ready, get started!"

4. **FEAR OF LOSING CONTROL.** Most adults see the fantasy world of children as something they will outgrow, yet it's adults who live in a fantasy world—one in which we erroneously believe we are in control. In reality, the only thing we can control is how we respond to life's circumstances. Since we can't lose control we never had, why do we spend so much energy seeking to control events outside ourselves? When we let go of that desire for control, we can start to tap into our creativity for new ideas and approaches.

Pushing Your Thinking

- Consider a recent or current issue that you face. What fear could be limiting your thinking about the problem and its possible solutions?
- What is the source of that fear?
- What new opportunities or options might appear if you suspended your fears?

Is it the message or the messenger?

In the 1960s, philosopher Marshall McLuhan wrote a best-selling book, *The Medium is the Massage: An Inventory of Effects*.[3] In it, he presents the case that a technological medium, in influencing how a message is perceived, becomes part of the content of that message; it is impossible to separate the two. Building on McLuhan's theory, I believe the perceptions we have about messengers influence how we interpret their messages in everyday discourse.

In political discourse, the public vacillates between prioritizing a candidate's clarity and platform and elevating candidates for their sincerity. Do we vote for people for what they say they believe, or do we vote for them because we *believe* what they say?

In everyday life there is a similar set of questions. Do I agree with what you say, or do I find you believable? If you are like me, your belief in someone being authentic supersedes what he or she says.

One cannot mimic authenticity. We judge the content of the message, largely, by the story we have about the messenger. If we perceive the messenger as honest, sincere, and like us, then we are more inclined to have a favorable reaction to the message.

Conversely, if we hold a negative story about the messenger, it doesn't matter what he or she says—we are inclined to disagree or dismiss it, sometimes even before the message is articulated.

Your message and intent may be noble and relevant, but the story each listener has about you will influence what he or she hears and how the person interprets your meaning.

In everyday conversations, then, it is neither the message nor the messenger that's most important; rather, the story we have about the messenger determines the message we hear.

Pushing Your Thinking

- What stories do others have about you?

- How might those stories alter their interpretation of your message from your intent?

- What can you do to revise the stories about you so your messages can be heard more clearly and as you intend them to be heard?

Are you a good listener?

Many of us were taught how to speak effectively, but I'm not sure if we are ever taught how to listen effectively. And yet, every good conversation begins with good listening. Is listening a natural skill or can it be learned? We can all identify a good listener—that go-to person when we need advice, need to understand a situation better, or just want someone to hear us. We think of listening as a passive activity, but effective or active listening takes time, practice, and dedication. Active listening is a communication technique. It requires that the listener fully concentrate, understand, respond to, and remember what is being said—not something most of us are good at. Being a good listener is an invaluable skill that can help us to see the world through the eyes of others. Here are seven tips for effective active listening.[4]

1. **BE FULLY PRESENT; DON'T BE DISTRACTED.** This one is tough right out of the gate. Our lives are filled with clutter, to-do lists, and problems to solve. Being present for someone else requires leaving these distractions at the door, setting them aside for attention later.

2. **DISARM YOUR HEARING FILTERS.** We listen through filters formed by our past experiences, biases, and the stories we have about the speaker. These filters often distort our objectivity and prevent empathetic listening. We first need to recognize our filters and then disarm them.

3. **BE PATIENT, DON'T INTERRUPT, AND RESIST THE TEMPTATION TO SPEAK.** We often start formulating a response before the speaker has finished, but listening requires our full attention. Too often we make the mistake of believing that the speaker wants a response. That little voice in our head likes to evaluate what we are hearing, but the speaker may just want us to listen.

4. **LISTEN WITH YOUR EYES AND EARS.** Listening goes beyond spoken words. Pay attention to the speaker's tone, cadence, body language, posture, and facial expressions. Visuals can amplify and clarify what is being said.

5. **ASK CLARIFYING QUESTIONS; TRY TO IDENTIFY THE "WHY" AND THE "WHAT".** Speakers want you to understand what they're saying. If something they say is unclear to you, inquire for more information. Ask open-ended questions when you need more information to better understand the "why" in addition to the "what."

6. **MAKE EYE CONTACT AND ENCOURAGE WITH BODY LANGUAGE.** Making regular eye contact lets the speaker know you're attentive and engaged, rather than bored or distracted. Be aware of your own nonverbal cues too: leaning forward, nodding your head, and smiling all send the signal that you're listening.

7. **RESIST THE TEMPTATION TO OFFER HELP UNTIL ASKED.** Some people think that when they're listening, they should find a quick and easy solution to the person's problem. Instead, focus on absorbing everything that's being said. Wait for a request before you offer help.

If you're a problem solver like me, you'll likely have a hard time with tip 7—and I'm still working on 1–6 too. We spend more time listening than speaking, and yet many of us aren't good at either. Listening takes time, practice, and dedication. A lot can be gained by learning when to stay quiet. Silence can be uncomfortable, which is why we often try to fill it. Good listeners are comfortable with the discomfort of silence.

Pushing Your Thinking

- Do you know a great listener? What makes the person so adept at listening?
- Which listening attributes do you excel at?
  Which need attention?
- What might you hear differently if you improved your listening skills?
- Who might seek your advice if you improved your listening skills?

Do you know the different shades of yes?

Have you ever asked permission and received a "yes," only to discover that it wasn't really the yes you thought it was? This may seem like a strange question. We think of most decisions as being binary—yes or no. But while a "no" is fairly clear-cut, a yes can be more ambiguous.

Consider this common scenario: it is dinnertime, and 14-year-old Lauren asks, "Hey, Mom, can I go to the mall with Sally tonight?" Mom replies, "Okay, yes." What has Mom just agreed to? Did they agree on how Lauren was going to get there, what time she should be home, or who else would be going? Mom just gave her teenager a "soft yes."

We encounter soft yeses all the time, and a soft yes is only a problem if we mistakenly interpret it as a hard yes. A hard yes is clear and definitive without any conditions attached.

I've come across at least four variations of a soft yes:

- **UNINFORMED YES.** This is a yes given without consideration to the implications
- **QUALIFIED YES.** A yes given with an unexpressed set of "only if" conditions
- **POLITE YES.** A yes given to appease the requester and when a no seems disrespectful or will hurt feelings
- **CLUELESS YES.** A yes given when you really don't understand what is being asked but are embarrassed to seek clarification

Offering a soft yes can be dangerous, especially when given to teen-aged children or when it involves money. Receiving a soft yes and misinterpreting it as a hard yes can be equally dangerous because of the mismatch of expectations.

By now you might be wondering if there is a soft no. My experience is that most adults consider a no a no, especially if repeated several times, whereas children hear every no as a soft no. They learn early on how to wear down repeated responses of no until they get a soft yes—which they will act on, promptly, like a hard yes.

Why can't life be simpler? Wasn't there a time when a yes meant yes and a no meant no? Probably not, and that is a soft no.

Pushing Your Thinking

- Do you remember a situation in which you received a soft yes but interpreted it as a hard yes? What were the consequences?

- Have there been situations with adults in which you gave a soft yes but it was interpreted as a hard yes? What were the consequences?

- What can you do to better distinguish between soft and hard yeses?

Should you be aware of your strengths?

We all have different portfolios of strengths and weaknesses. Several best-selling books focus on developing and using our strengths. Sometimes, though, focusing on those strengths can lead us astray and even undermine our success.

BE AWARE OF YOUR STRENGTHS. We need to be acutely aware of both our strengths and our weaknesses, and I've always been a believer that we should put more time into developing our strengths than improving our weaknesses. Leaders are people who have distinguished themselves through their strengths, having maximized their natural skills. Of course, we all have weaknesses, but if we focus on our weaknesses, we won't have the time or energy to excel at our strengths. Now, that doesn't mean we should ignore our weaknesses. Rather, we should be aware of the circumstances during which they will significantly limit our ability to accomplish our intentions, and focus on our strengths the rest of the time.

Now I am going to state something that may seem counterintuitive:

We are more likely to get into trouble by misusing a strength than by stumbling from a weakness.

When faced with a difficult situation, we are likely to return to the strengths that have served us well in the past. Like overusing a muscle, reverting to these strengths becomes a knee-jerk reaction. In many cases this works for us, but occasionally we misuse a strength—that is, the strength has no relevance to the situation, but we employ it anyway out of instinct. Before we are aware of it, we've made things worse. Unaware of what is happening, we might even respond by drawing on the same strength again, only to dig a deeper hole. Look behind the story of one of your work failures, and I suspect you will find a misused strength.

When the going gets tough, be aware of your instinctive response.

Don't get me wrong—your strengths are what set you apart. But examine each situation carefully and make a conscious decision as to what actions are appropriate and productive before you react.

Pushing Your Thinking

- Do you know what strengths distinguish you?
  How have those strengths served your success in the past?

- Can you remember a situation when you employed the strength out of instinct and found yourself in trouble?

- Why did that happen? What might you have done differently?

Are you a habitual evaluator?

The other day four friends were walking in a park enjoying the beautiful weather.

NATALIA COMMENTED: Look at the blue sky with the beautiful clouds. Isn't it wonderful?

STEPHEN SAID: I prefer a clear sky. The clouds are distracting.

HENRY SAID: I think the clouds look threatening. It looks like it's going to rain soon.

ANNA REMAINED QUIET, BUT THOUGHT TO HERSELF: Natalia is such an idealist. Who has time to think about the sky? I need to get back to doing real work.

In this simple example, Natalia's pleasant observation and rhetorical question were greeted with scrutiny and appraisal.

Isn't that the way it is? Too often we listen to conversations through a filter of measurement, judgment, and evaluation.

Do I agree or disagree? Yes or no? Is it right or wrong?
Is it good or bad? Is it better than or worse than?

You have probably been in a meeting where someone was making an observation when another person disagreed before the sentence was completed. That was probably a habitual evaluator.

These people stop listening to what is being said and start forming their response before developing a full understanding of the point, making their evaluations, however relevant, much less palatable.

Do we need to be evaluators? What's the worst that would happen if we suspended our instinct to pass judgment and just listened?

Some (or even many) things just are; they don't need evaluation. We might even learn to appreciate both the blue sky and the clouds in the process.

Pushing Your Thinking

- Do you listen and see the world through a filter of evaluation? Why do you think that is?
- What filters influence how you make those evaluations?
- What would it take to suspend the filters and listen without evaluation?
- Do you experience others evaluating you, your comments and actions?

Are you strong enough to be vulnerable?

We are all vulnerable, but most of us don't like to show or admit it. We equate vulnerability with weakness, and we don't want to appear weak. In fact, we put a lot of energy into not appearing weak, and we say and do things to try to convince others that we are strong even when we are not.

Reflecting on my own experience, I've identified five areas that are common sources of vulnerability:

- **ADMITTING I DON'T KNOW.** It can be scary to admit we don't have the answer, but the older we get and the more we learn, the more we realize we can never know it all. Admitting when we don't know, rather than bluffing, builds trust and respect.

- **OWNING MY FAILURES OR MISTAKES.** None of us wants to fail, but we all make mistakes every day. We often look for reasons and excuses for our mistakes, but learning to take responsibility for them is a sign of maturity and confidence.

- **SAYING I'M SORRY.** Acknowledging we were wrong, either with our actions or with their impact, can make us feel vulnerable and defensive. Apologizing is extraordinarily difficult for only two words, but offering "I apologize" authentically builds relationships, fosters completeness, and underscores the value of honesty.

- **ASKING FOR HELP.** If you think you are supposed to know, you will be reluctant to ask for help—even when you need it—for fear of being seen as inadequate or incompetent. Learning from those with more experience, though, is the best way to build your skillset and develop new professional contacts.

- **ACKNOWLEDGING FEARS.** We all have fears, and one of our greatest is that others will see them. Regardless of how much we try to hide them, though, our fears will eventually become visible. But what are we so afraid of? Most people will see our fears as a basic element of our humanity, not a weakness.

When any of these common events trigger our vulnerabilities, we're likely to get defensive and may even act out. We pretend like we know. We blame others for our mistakes. We stay the course without asking for help. We make-believe that we're fearless. Yet when others allow their vulnerabilities to show, we see them as human, with imperfections. In some situations, we even admire those who display vulnerability as strong and authentic. Embrace and be relaxed about your moments of vulnerability. You may discover a new strength.

Pushing Your Thinking

- Where and when do you feel vulnerable?
- What do you do to hide your vulnerabilities?
- What is the worst thing that could happen if others saw your vulnerabilities?
- What is the best thing that could happen if others saw your vulnerabilities?

Are you limited by your fears?

We all have fears about ourselves and our interactions with others. Many of us tend to keep our fears private. We believe that exposing our fears makes us vulnerable. Of course, we are all vulnerable, and our vulnerabilities make us human. It is fear that stifles our thinking and actions: it creates indecisiveness that can result in stagnation.

Dr. Manfred F. R. Kets de Vries, professor from INSEAD, has written about how fear hinders success.[5] I'm not a psychologist, but it doesn't take a PhD to recognize our fears. Here are ten common ones:

1. **LOSING CONTROL.** We want to be in control, or at least believe we're in control. Many of us spend more time lamenting the things we can't control than thinking about the things we can: our choices.

2. **UNKNOWN.** Much is unknown—some good and some not so good. But if we knew what the future would bring, we would be so preoccupied trying to prevent bad things from happening we'd forget to enjoy today. Instead of fearing the future, we might be wise to remember the past "unknowns" that surprised us and made us happy.

3. **BEING WRONG.** We want to be right. Being wrong may indicate that we're not as smart as we think we are. And guess what? We often aren't.

4. **NOT KNOWING.** For some of us, worse than being wrong is not knowing. In fact, we may prefer to be wrong than admit we don't know. Remember, Confucius said, "True wisdom is knowing what you don't know."

5. **CONFLICT.** Most of us avoid conflict because conflict is unpleasant. Over time, suppressing conflict results in an accumulation of negative feelings that we carry into the future.

6. **REJECTION.** Most of us want to be liked and accepted. Our fear of rejection can drive us to avoid situations in which we believe that we might experience some form of rejection, limiting our opportunities.

7. **FAILURE.** While it is true we learn from failure, of course we would prefer not to fail in the first place. Focusing on avoiding failure, though, prevents us from taking the risks necessary for learning new skills and exploring novel ideas.

8. **BEING FOUND OUT.** Feeling vulnerable can easily lead to anxiety about being "found out." The "impostor syndrome" is often used to describe high-achieving individuals who have difficulty acknowledging their accomplishments and fear being exposed as "frauds." They spend so much time playing defense—trying to hide their perceived inadequacies—that they fail to celebrate their success.

9. **NOT MEASURING UP.** We often compare ourselves to others, or to some unrealistic ideal. We can easily find a skill for which we are "less than" when we compare ourselves to others. Yet those who believe they do "not measure up" are often high achievers in the eyes of others.

10. **SUCCESS.** As strange as it might seem, some people fear success. They achieve great success and recognition yet believe that they don't deserve it, that somehow their success is misplaced. This self-deception of unworthiness can easily get in the way of future success.

So, if we all have fears, should we be living in a state of fear? Absolutely not! We can be aware of our fears without being a prisoner to them. When we acknowledge our fears, we can better understand why we behave the way we do. Over time some fears will diminish as drivers of our actions.

Pushing Your Thinking

- Which fears do you experience most often?
- What is the source of those fears?
- What opportunities might be created, or how might you behave, if you didn't have those fears?
- What can you do to face and move past your fears?

What are the benefits of fear?

One of the greatest discoveries a man makes, one of his great surprises, is to find he can do what he was afraid he couldn't do.
—HENRY FORD

We know our fears can hold us back in many ways, and we certainly have plenty of reasons to be fearful, but can our fears be harnessed to benefit us? At the most basic level, fear is a survival instinct: it is a natural and necessary reaction when we sense threats or danger. Although we generally think about fear as an unpleasant emotion, I got to thinking about what its benefits might be. Here are three thoughts:

1. **FEAR PROVIDES INSTANT FOCUS.** Fear snaps us into being present. It is impossible to multitask when we're afraid; emails, text messages, and other daily distractions fall by the wayside as we focus on the threat. This clarity of thought can improve our decision making and help us prioritize the steps to success.

2. **FEAR IS A SIGN WE MIGHT BE DOING SOMETHING IMPORTANT.** Nothing great can be accomplished without facing a fear. Olympic athletes, great actors, and successful businesspeople all feel pressure, anxiety, and fear. That's part of what makes them great: they are doing something worthy of fear. Each of us remembers moments in our lives—applying for a promotion, proposing to our spouse, chasing a dream, starting a business— when we faced deep personal fears. Those were moments of truth that defined our character.

3. **FEAR BUILDS CONFIDENCE.** When we do something that scares us and overcome a fear, we become stronger. Self-confidence is the result of having successfully survived a risk. The more fears we face, and the more successes we have, the greater our belief in ourselves and our confidence in challenging our next fear.

I read recently that without fear we might be "stuck on the treadmill of mediocrity."[6] Now that's something to be afraid of.

Pushing Your Thinking

- When was the last time you took a risk and overcame a fear? Did it build your self-confidence?

- Are your fears increasing or decreasing?

- How do we learn to harness our fears and use them constructively?

Are you a good sense-maker?

We live in a complex, fast-paced world where events and experiences often don't make sense. Yet we want to make sense of the world around us. In particular, we want to understand why things happen the way they do so we can anticipate and prepare for the future. We hope that the world is rational—that is, that there is a cause–effect order to life's events. This is especially true for negative occurrences; we prefer not to believe bad things happen randomly. While I'm far from an expert on "sense-making," I have found it useful to ask myself three simple questions to help guide me in understanding my world: What's so? So what? Now what?

WHAT'S SO? To understand the world around us, we must first observe what is going on. Unfortunately, many of us are so busy and distracted "doing" that we have a hard time observing. We also suffer from "observation dementia," where we are so overwhelmed with information that our capacity to remember and process is limited. Unless what we see has immediate relevance, we are likely to forget it. As Yogi Berra said, "You can observe a lot by just watching."

SO WHAT? Keen observation is necessary but not sufficient—we still want to derive meaning from what we see today and expect to experience in the future. In most cases, a single observation by itself reveals only a small piece of the puzzle, but our tendency is to respond quickly, before we fully understand what it could mean or whether a response is even appropriate. A wider perspective is needed to recognize patterns, discern trends, and understand the potential implications of what we see. Part of our interpretation of what we see in the present is based on our past experiences, which we also use to try to predict the future consequences of today's events.

NOW WHAT? When we encounter new information or a new event, our instincts prompt us to act or react, especially if we think we are approaching a crisis. However, if it's difficult to observe what's going on and easy to debate what it might mean, we can imagine the difficulties in deciding what, if anything, to do. Some will want to learn from similar events in the past: "I've seen this before, and we should do this." While repetition provides comfort, a change in the context can easily lead us to employ an inappropriate strategy. Oftentimes, a delayed response is the most thoughtful response.

Pushing Your Thinking

- Are you a good sense-maker? How do you know?
- At what aspect of sense-making do you excel?
- How did you develop that capability?
- What responsibility do you have to others to make sense of events or others' actions?

What makes you happy?

Happiness is personal. Your sources of happiness are likely different from anyone else's, especially your children's. Two researchers, Amit Bhattacharjee and Cassie Mogilner, have researched the topic and written a paper, "Happiness from Ordinary and Extraordinary Experiences."[7]

The researchers found that age—particularly the differences between people above or below the mid-30s mark—played a key role in what made individuals happy.

Bhattacharjee and Mogilner conclude that "younger people who view their future as extensive gain more happiness from extraordinary experiences." As people get older and more aware of their mortality, ordinary experiences become increasingly associated with happiness. "You take the day-to-day stuff for granted when you have plenty of days left for experiences," they write.

The researchers define ordinary experiences as "those that are common, frequent, and within the realm of everyday life," such as sharing a meal with family or friends. Extraordinary experiences, on the other hand, are defined as being "uncommon, infrequent and going beyond the realm of everyday life," such as a trip around the world.

The role of self-definition was one of the most surprising results of the study. "Irrespective of how old you are, experiences that are self-defining make you happy. But as you get older, there is a shift in what experiences you use to define yourself," they note. "Even amidst the dizzying, infinite array of possible experiences, our findings suggest that there is underlying order. A happy life includes both the extraordinary and the ordinary, and the central question is not only which, but when."

No matter where we are in life, therefore, we engage in activities and experiences that can bring us joy. Unfortunately, some people are so consumed being unhappy they miss the events that could be a source of happiness for them. We need happiness to sustain us, though, so the next time you find yourself happy, cherish the moment, day, or week. You might be surprised at how enriched those memories will make you feel.

Pushing Your Thinking

- Think of an ordinary event that made you happy. What was it that evoked the happiness?

- Now think of an extraordinary event that made you happy. Did you recognize your happiness at the time?

- Which event provided greater happiness?

- Would that same ordinary experience have made you happy 20 years ago? Why or why not?

- What ordinary experiences today make you happy?

Pushing the Edge of Possibility

As our life experiences shape our thinking, our thinking determines our beliefs about what's possible. Over time, we develop a set of assumptions about why things are the way they are. We use these assumptions to make sense of events—those that directly affect us, as well as those that we merely observe. As time passes, our assumptions fade from the foreground of our awareness into our subconsciousness, where they continue to operate silently.

These assumptions determine the boundaries of possibility we observe. For some, the boundaries appear broad, creating a worldview of abundance. For others, the boundaries seem narrow and limiting. To broaden our beliefs about what's possible, we must bring any constraining assumptions up from our subconscious and into the foreground to challenge them.

These assumptions aren't artificial—they're due to our life experiences. Challenging them involves three steps. First, we must identify the assumptions we have, to determine what effect they're having on our perception and interpretation of events. Second, we need to identify the specific experiences that formed our assumptions, to figure out why we believe them. Finally, we must examine whether those assumptions have any relevance and benefit for us today and release any that don't serve us well.

This section poses questions and offers insights that can help you challenge your assumptions and expand the boundaries of what you believe is possible. Consider the questions and reflect on your answers. You might discover a new world of possibilities.

Are you a critic or a champion?

Every day we hear debates for and against positions, ideas, and actions, but lately the balance of conversation seems to have tipped heavily toward criticism. It's easy to be a critic. After all, we're all human, with many imperfections. With so much criticism in the air, are the champions going underground? If so, how can we help them come out from the shadows and stand up for what they believe?

Champions advocate publicly for causes and values they believe in, opening themselves up to criticism. We can easily find something "wrong" with any champion's position; if a cause needs a champion, by definition, barriers and challenges are associated with it. Champions who take firm stands often succeed in mobilizing supportive followers. Some potential champions, though, fearing the inevitable criticism, aren't confident enough to advocate publicly, and they keep good ideas to themselves.

In daily life, we encounter many things with which we disagree. Many of us keep our disagreement to ourselves to avoid conflict. Others enjoy an argument independent of the issue; they seem to make a sport of criticizing. Some just want to prove another person "wrong," while a few are primarily interested in denigrating, ridiculing, or even demonizing those they disagree with. Put two of these critics in a room and you'll likely see limited listening, with each person talking past the other.

By now, you may have concluded that I'm being a critic of the critics, but don't get me wrong—we're all critics and champions at different points in time. In fact, champions need critics to help them understand the nuances of their cause, to test their commitment and understanding, and to find effective ways of engaging others.

Without champions who advocate, we would stagnate in the status quo. Without critics who challenge our thinking, we would see no improvement. Without mutual respect, tolerance, and civility, we would have no learning or innovation.

Pushing Your Thinking

- What issue do you care about enough to champion?
- What holds you back from advocating for your beliefs?
- How can you apply your criticism to support a champion?

Do you know your purpose?

It's a pretty profound question, yet many of us go through life never considering our purpose. Often, it isn't until we're confronted with our mortality that the purpose of life enters our consciousness. Age, illness, and loss all bring the impermanence of life into sharp focus. In those situations, we might find ourselves asking, "Why am I here? What do I have to offer? Have I made a difference?"

To find your purpose, start by looking within. Examine your dreams and aspirations. Reflect on your life and consider what brought you the most joy and in which moments you felt most alive. Do you see any common threads, a connection that might lead you to your purpose? Don't be afraid to draw a blank—just because you haven't discovered your purpose doesn't mean you don't have one. Understanding your purpose is a deeply personal matter and usually requires lengthy reflection. For some people, the question may feel overly emotional or even a little silly, but the rewards are great. Before you begin probing, ask yourself, "If I knew I had a purpose, how would I act differently?"

We explore this question in my leadership course, in a module focused on "passion and purpose." In it, each student approaches three to five friends, relatives, or colleagues and asks if they have discovered their purpose in life. If that person answers yes, the student asks what the purpose is and how he or she discovered it. The students then summarize their experiences, highlighting any common themes that surfaced during their inquiries.

Almost universally the students find at least one person who knows his or her purpose and is eager to discuss it. They recount that the discussion is always very positive, nonthreatening, and high-energy, and that those who know their purpose live with great passion. While the paths to this realization are all different, people often point to overcoming adversity in their lives as the source of their self-aware-ness. Students come away with a deeper understanding of the other person, as well as the source of that person's happiness. Although I don't ask the students to describe their own purpose in life, the assignment gives them the nudge and inspiration to reflect on it.

Pushing Your Thinking

Consider asking three to five of your friends about their purpose in life. If that feels too awkward, you can engage in a simple exercise developed by author and motivational speaker Steve Pavlina[8]:

1. Take out a blank sheet of paper
2. Write at the top, "What is my true purpose in life?"
3. Write an answer (any answer) that pops into your head. It doesn't have to be a complete sentence; a short phrase is fine.
4. Repeat step 3 until you write the answer that makes you cry. This is your purpose.

Pavlina says that discovering your purpose is the easy part. The hard part is working on yourself to the point where you become that purpose. Take a moment to reflect on how to add more passion to your life. You can start becoming the person you were meant to be.

Where has our tolerance gone?

We still remember the hate murders of Charleston, South Carolina, a racist act of violence against twelve loving people, a community, and a nation. Although we would like to believe prejudice and bigotry are in our nation's past, we know that even today many are emboldened by their hate. Tragedies like Charleston should prompt each of us to examine where we stand on the issue of tolerance. Do we consider ourselves tolerant? Are we ever intolerant? If so, of what?

What do we mean by tolerance? It's not enough to merely acknowledge another person's right to exist. Tolerance is respect, acceptance, and appreciation for the richness of human differences. It is a mindset that doesn't distinguish whether someone is "like us" or not. Tolerance is a moral responsibility.

It's common to be uncertain of people who are different from us. Whether it's race, religion, disability, national origin, socioeconomic status, sexual preference, or some other variance in the human condition, we find it difficult to identify with those we see as different. Too often, we fear things we don't understand, and this fear makes us uncomfortable and suspicious around people who don't appear the same as us. To feel safer, we create groups, assign labels, and build walls—we distance ourselves from "the other."

Learning tolerance can seem daunting, but it doesn't have to be difficult. Although we may believe our differences separate us from one another, when we look closely, we'll discover we have more in common than not—after all, we all want to be healthy, to be happy, to be able to care for our families. Respecting the fundamental humanity of all people, even those we don't understand, will make practicing tolerance much easier.

The families of those slain in Charleston offered forgiveness in the face of the worst kind of intolerance. We can't imagine the horror that they faced, but their grace has touched the hearts of us all. Let's echo their message of love by showing ourselves, our children, and one another what tolerance looks like.

Pushing Your Thinking

- When is your tolerance most challenged? How do you act?
- How can we model tolerance for children?
- What can we learn from children about tolerance and acceptance?

Are you energized?

We seem to have an energy crisis. I'm not thinking about coal, oil, or even solar—rather, I'm talking about personal energy. Personal energy is a combination of our intellectual, emotional, and physical energy. Conventional wisdom tells us that eating well, getting enough sleep, and exercising will improve our energy levels, but is that enough? No matter how healthy our lifestyle is, daily interactions and responsibilities can still drain our energy reservoir dry. Amy Martinez, a senior faculty member with the Center for Creative Leadership, has written about managing our personal energy.[9]

When we decide how to spend our time, or whom to spend it with, we are also deciding how to spend our energy. We gain energy from activities that give us pleasure and lose energy from engaging in stressful situations. Energy also constantly flows when we're communicating with others. While we draw energy from supportive friends and family, on occasion we have to interact with "energy vampires." These people seem to suck away our good feelings with their narrow views and relentless naysaying. While we won't be able to rid our lives of all energy vampires, we don't have to accommodate them by accepting their invitations to arguments or responding to their negativity.

Many times, we expend unnecessary energy worrying about things outside our control. We regret past decisions that may not have served us well and carry those memories as burdens that sap our energy reserves. Happiness today is more important than righting the injustices of the past or preventing potential crises of the future—personal energy is limited; don't waste it on regrets or worries.

Learn to be your own best advocate and surround yourself with people who make you feel better about yourself, rather than those who deplete your energy. Participate in activities and volunteer for projects that give you confidence and a sense of fulfillment, and decline those invitations that leave you feeling drained. Remember, you can choose how and where to focus your energy—you can live in a way that increases your energy rather than exhausts it. Be energized and be happy.

Pushing Your Thinking

- What is your energy level first thing each day?
- Who or what gives you energy during the day? Who or what depletes it?
- In conversations, do you provide energy or drain it from others? Why might that be the case?
- What can you start or stop doing that will increase your personal energy?

Is the American Dream still alive?

The American Dream is a set of ideals in which everyone has access to opportunity and social mobility through hard work, unobstructed by artificial barriers. James Truslow Adams, in his 1931 book, *The Epic of America*, stated this about the American Dream:

> The dream is of a land in which life should be better and richer and fuller for everyone, with opportunity for each according to ability or achievement. It is not a dream of motor cars and high wages merely, but a dream of social order in which each man and each woman shall be able to attain to the fullest stature of which they are innately capable, and be recognized by others for what they are, regardless of the fortuitous circumstances of birth or position.[10]

Today many people believe the American Dream has become elusive for the middle class, not to mention an ideal far beyond the reach of the poor, who often must work two or more jobs to ensure their families' survival. Sadly, it may be true.

AN IMMIGRANT'S STORY. My grandparents came to the United States more than 100 years ago, fleeing oppression from the government in the Ottoman Empire. They were threatened because of their Armenian heritage and their Christian religion. It's hard for me to imagine them boarding a boat for a distant port with few personal belongings. They braved a ferocious ocean, learned a new language, lived in an unfamiliar culture, and embraced a new country, all to give their descendants a happy life filled with opportunities. None of my grandparents lived to see me graduate from college or visited my home in Massachusetts. My story is not unique. My grandparents' belief in the American Dream stretched beyond their own lives.

Like the air we breathe, we take the American Dream for granted. But even if we are several generations removed from the struggles of our immigrant ancestors, we—as well as the generations that will follow us—need to keep in mind the courage and sacrifices made by those who came before us.

IN SEARCH OF THE AMERICAN DREAM. Today we are the stewards of the American Dream. It is our responsibility to provide hope to those seeking a better life, whether they're new immigrants to our shores or citizens who've struggled against social and economic disadvantages. Recognize that their hope is simple: a better life for themselves and their descendants. Look for any opportunities to make the American Dream a real possibility for them.

Do you want to find the American Dream? Don't look to Washington or to any political candidate—look in the mirror. You are the American Dream that your ancestors sought and today's immigrants hope for.

Pushing Your Thinking

- What does the American Dream mean to you?
- What have you achieved that would make your ancestors proud? What do you think would make them happy for the hardships they experienced or the sacrifices they made for your future?
- What can you do to help others achieve their American Dream?

Can a "Dreamer" realize the American Dream?

"Eduardo" is a "Dreamer"—the son of an undocumented immigrant who was brought to the United States as a child.

EDUARDO'S STORY. Eduardo's mother came to the United States from Central America in 1995 with two-year-old Eduardo and his six-year-old sister. His mother had been a journalist in her native country but, fearing for her life amidst violent political turmoil, she fled.

In the United States, their family lived in a sanctuary city. Eduardo grew up surrounded by Mexicans and Central Americans who'd escaped drug and cartel violence, families from the Middle East who'd fled war, as well as Africans, Eastern Europeans, and Asians all in search of the American Dream. Eduardo had to adapt to the cultural norms of his friends and neighbors. He described his challenge to me: "I had no choice but to maintain a positive attitude because it was either take advantage of the opportunity here or go back to a place that would likely see us dead within a month. We had no choice."

SEEKING ACCEPTANCE. One evening Eduardo and his girlfriend were sitting at a bar having a private conversation about the 2016 presidential election, while they were waiting to be seated for dinner. A man overheard them and started hurling racial slurs, confronting them and declaring that Eduardo should not get too comfortable, he would soon be going "back where he came from." Eduardo chose not to confront the man and left the restaurant with his girlfriend, saddened that even today, after 22 years, he is still not accepted by everyone in the United States.

Then Eduardo remembered that his mother had brought two small children, with only the clothes on their backs, to this country in search of a better life. Eduardo reflected on how strong his mother had been despite many encounters like this. He reminded himself of her pride at his recent graduation from college with honors. "No one can take away my self-esteem or my dignity. If I've made it this far in my life without some people wanting me here, I'm not going to stop now. I deserve to be here as much as anyone else seeking a better life." The American Dream: hope and opportunity for everyone.

PERSEVERANCE AND STRENGTH. I had the opportunity to meet Eduardo, now a mathematician, last year. I asked him what advice his mother gave him growing up. "Never give up. Be resilient. Work past your fears," she said. That's advice that we can all use.

Pushing Your Thinking

* Who are the Dreamers in your life?
* How close are they to realizing the American Dream?
* What can you do to support them?

Are you as smart as a kindergartner?

Remember the television game show *Are You Smarter Than a 5th Grader*? When watching the show, I usually scored higher than the contestants, but I rarely knew as much as the children. That got me wondering: Am I as smart as a kindergartner?

Years ago, I read Robert Fulghum's popular book, *All I Really Need to Know I Learned in Kindergarten*.[11] Recently, I found it tucked away on my bookshelf, dusted it off, and reread it. In today's chaotic, challenging world, his points resonated even more deeply with me than before. I looked at a few of the book's themes to see if, as adults, we still practice what we were taught.

SHARE EVERYTHING. As children, we were constantly being reminded to share. As adults, we like to accumulate "toys" just as children do, but we can be even more possessive of them. We have all heard someone say, "These are mine. Go get your own," "I worked hard for my things. You can't have them," or even, "Mine is bigger and better than yours." If we were more willing to share, though, we might be surprised by how much we are offered in return.

PLAY FAIR. Do you remember, in kindergarten, when recess was all about playing? There was no scoreboard then; it was just about having fun. As we got older, many of us became so obsessed with winning we might even cheat or put the other person down to come out on top. Playing fair means playing by the rules, respecting others, and enjoying the milk and cookies at the end of the day. As adults, playing fair adds another dimension to our happiness because we know our success is achieved honorably.

CLEAN UP YOUR OWN MESS. We learned in kindergarten that messes are part of life. We were taught to care for our space and not to point fingers. We learned that acknowledging accidents and cleaning up the messes we made were correct ways to handle our mistakes. As adults, many of us are too eager to blame someone else when things go wrong, when we should be taking responsibility to fix what we can.

SAY YOU'RE SORRY WHEN YOU HURT SOMEONE. Most of us learned "please" and "thank you" at an early age. We learned that respecting other people's feelings is of paramount importance. But the words "I'm sorry" seem to get harder and harder to say as we grow older. Remember, it's not always about how we feel or what we mean, but how the other person feels because of our actions. Impact is more important than intent—apologizing when we've caused pain can go a long way toward mending relationships.

WHEN YOU GO OUT INTO TRAFFIC, HOLD HANDS AND STICK TOGETHER. How many times have we seen young boys and girls out on a field trip, holding hands? Children hold hands to stay safe. If adults could learn to see the common elements that bind different people together, and what we could gain from broad, trust-based teamwork, we would be less afraid of holding hands and more inclined to stick together.

It seems in many ways the kindergartners have a lot to teach us.

Pushing Your Thinking

- Which of these themes is the most relevant for you today? How can you put it into practice?
- What new possibilities could your practice create in your relationships, in your career, or for your overall happiness?
- How can we model these behaviors for children so they continue the practices they learn in kindergarten?

Are you gracious when receiving gifts from others?

How many of us were told, when we were young, "it is better to give than to receive"? This life lesson was intended to teach us that generosity is one of life's greatest virtues and to prevent us from becoming selfish and entitled. On the surface it seems like a faultless message, but is it universally true? For every giver, after all, there must be a receiver. Should we refuse to receive gifts for fear of being judged selfish? Isn't there value in both giving and receiving?

Such a simple and generally accepted truth now appears more complicated under closer examination. We'd better start by defining our terms. When we think of "givers," we imagine people who go out of their way to help without expecting anything in return. The term "receiver," on the other hand, really seems to appear only in football. In life, we often substitute the term "taker," but "taker" sounds much more active and selfish than "receiver." Takers, we imagine, are people who feel entitled to get as much as possible from others and to give back as little as they can in return.

Yet, is receiving another person's offering—"taking" their gift—truly a selfish act? If you are like me, you probably have more practice and comfort in giving than receiving. I can easily start to feel a little guilty when I'm on the receiving end of an exchange.

Several years ago I had an extended stay in the hospital, during which time I had to learn how to receive without guilt. In fact, receiving became a regular part of my life because I was no longer physically independent. Things I used to do on my own, such as opening doors or reaching for items in a store, now required the assistance of others. Since then, I've learned to accept these "gifts of assistance" with gratitude and a thank-you, free from embarrassment Those gifts make my life a little easier, and I've discovered a heartfelt thank-you is, in fact, its own gift in return.

In life, we are all both givers and takers, and just as we ought to be generous with our giving, we should be generous in receiving. Givers feel most valuable when we accept their gifts graciously, embracing them in the spirit in which the gifts were offered. Thankful receiving is our gift to the giver.

Pushing Your Thinking

* Is it difficult for you to receive a gift or a compliment? If so, why?

* Do you silently squirm inside when someone offers a kind word or a present—or do you allow yourself to deeply receive the gift of kindness, caring, and connection?

* In your world, who are the genuine givers? Whose giving goes the most unrecognized? How can you acknowledge the giver?

* How do you decide whom to help—is it the person who needs the most, the person you can help the most, or some other reason?

Do you know when "good enough" is good enough?

Our society recognizes and rewards excellence. We may have strived for an A in school, practiced days upon days to nail an audition, or rewritten an essay umpteen times to get it right. Sports enthusiasts root for their local teams to win world championships and are disappointed when they fall short. But do we always need to strive for excellence?

What would happen if we only did what's "good enough"? Would we consider ourselves to be failing to satisfy a personal expectation?

GOOD, BETTER, OR BEST. Many of us interpret the evaluation of "good enough" as the reflection of a low-quality product or result. When shopping, we are often given a choice between good, better, and best, with "good" being the lowest quality and least expensive option. For those of us who strive for excellence, "good enough" sounds uncomfortably close to "low quality," and it can be a difficult concept to embrace. None of us wants to act with "low quality," so we are prompted to look for ways to do better. This search for "better quality" can easily become a cycle with no logical end of "best."

ADVICE FOR PERFECTIONISTS. Those of us who are perfectionists need to learn when and where to expend that extra effort for excellence. Perfectionists tend to dismiss any of their work that's less than optimal. But think about it—we must make judgments on how we use our time; not everything warrants extra effort to achieve marginal improvements. Time is a scarce commodity, and few of us have the abundance of time to perfect everything we do. In some situations, 20 percent of the effort can produce 80 percent of the optimal result, and 80 percent may be enough for what's needed. Sometimes "good enough" is good enough. During those times, we need to declare victory and move on, lest we get caught chasing an elusive ideal.

Pushing Your Thinking

- How do you make judgments regarding the amount of effort appropriate to achieve a desired result or complete a task?

- When you give a task to others, do they understand your expectations regarding effort and quality? If not, how can you create clear alignment?

- How can a perfectionist learn that "good enough" is good enough?

Would you rather be approximately right or precisely wrong?

I recently came across this story:

> Malcolm Forbes once got lost floating for miles in one of his famous hot-air balloons. He finally landed in the middle of a cornfield. He spotted a man coming toward him and asked, "Sir, can you tell me where I am?" The man said, "Certainly, you are in a basket in a field of corn." Forbes said, "You must be a statistician." The man said, "That's amazing! How did you know that?" "Easy," said Forbes, "your information is concise, precise, and absolutely useless!"[12]

When faced with a tough decision, many of us choose to take the path for which we can accumulate the most supporting data and facts, but can data ever lead us down the wrong path? How do we handle facts that appear to be conflicting?

None of us wants to be wrong, and tough decisions don't have easy answers, but relying too heavily on data can be a mistake. Many of us believe that decisions must be worked on, worked on some more, and completely supported with hard data and evidence before action is taken. We tend to abide by the saying, "when in doubt, get more data." That approach can lead us to overthink our decisions and often undermines progress and innovation. Other people blindly believe what the data seem to say. Even though their analysis may not feel right, they silence their inner skeptics. They ignore their instincts and simply accept the assessment at face value. Because it can be uncomfortable to choose a path that just feels right, they prefer to take the path for which they have plenty of data instead—even if the data are irrelevant, incorrect, or even nonsensical.

The idea of following your instincts without regard for supporting evidence is not a common one. As humans, we gravitate toward decisions that offer high levels of certainty. We see safety in things that appear precise because we equate higher precision with increased certainty. Even though being approximately right is better than being precisely wrong, we still tend toward precision. Now, don't get the wrong impression. I'm not against data. I'm just suggesting that we may benefit from trusting ourselves more. I can't prove it with facts. It's just my instinct.

Pushing Your Thinking

- When was the last time you were precisely wrong?

- Did your instincts tell you to make a different decision? Why didn't you trust your instinct?

- Can you accept being approximately right rather than seeking precision in all your decisions? What compromises would you have to make in your thinking?

Are you obsessed with being right?

We all like to be right in our judgments, decisions, and actions. Whether it's winning an argument, correctly predicting an outcome, or recalling a fact someone else forgot, being right makes us feel good. My guess is that being right activates the pleasure center of our brains, which rewards us and encourages repetition. Given the choice between being right or being wrong, who would choose to be wrong?

WHAT IS *RIGHT* AND *WRONG*? The dictionary defines *right* as "conforming to facts or truth." Are someone's opinions or ideas right, though, just because they conform to a fact? If two diverging viewpoints each conform to the truth, is one more right than the other? By the way, whose truth are we talking about? Truth can be entirely subjective, as we interpret it through the filters of our own lives and experiences. How can we measure truth on a scale of right and wrong? Remember that facts change too, and what was right yesterday may be wrong today.

WHY THE INTENSE NEED TO BE RIGHT? "Being right" is different from making decisions that turn out to be right. "Being right" is more personal—some even consider it a part of their identity or an indication of their goodness. Needing to "be right" implies a need for publicity, a need to be validated by others. Chances are, our desire to be right is an ego thing. People stress themselves out because of their fear of appearing inadequate and embarrassment of being wrong.

BREAKING THE OBSESSION: A THREE-STEP PROCESS. To break your obsession with being right, try the following: the next time you know you're right in a disagreement, pause. Then employ the following three steps to help you consciously back off your ego's need to prove itself.

STEP 1: RECOGNIZE THAT YOUR EGO WANTS TO BE RIGHT. Notice how invested you are in being right, especially once you've stated your opinion publicly. Yes, it's difficult to change your position even when you know you should, but try letting it go. Let the other person believe he or she is right. Notice your reactions to letting the person believe he or she is right.

STEP 2: IMAGINE BEING IN THE OTHER PERSON'S SHOES AND SEEING WHAT'S GOING ON THROUGH THAT PERSON'S EYES. Pay attention to how attached you feel to your position. Of course, it's your opinion and you want it to be right, but what do you look like from the other person's perspective? Do you seem stubborn, arrogant, or even self-absorbed? Is that how you want to be experienced?

STEP 3: LISTEN TO THE OTHER PERSON'S VIEWPOINT AND IMAGINE THAT IT'S TRUE. Now this may sound hard, but try suspending your disbelief just for a moment. Trust me, the world won't collapse. There is so much to learn from listening with an open mind. People will start to react differently to you. You will feel more connected, and you may even learn new things, ideas that were closed off to you before.

I'm not claiming I'm right with this three-step approach, but I bet it will help you become more conscious of your natural desire to be right. Remember, while it may be nice to be right, it's better to be happy.

Pushing Your Thinking

- Are you obsessed with being right? Why?
- When was the last time you were certain you were right, only to discover you weren't?
- Next time you argue with your partner or your children, can you imagine they may be right (at least for a little while)?

What's the downside of managing expectations down?

Most of us learned the value of integrity when we were young. We saw that keeping our word and our promises strengthened friendships and impressed our parents. As adults, reliability and consistency continue to be valued by our friends and colleagues.

When we make a commitment, we create an expectation that we will fulfill on that commitment, like it is a promise. As such, we don't make commitments lightly, and we make no commitments that we do not intend to keep.

We learn to manage others' expectations of us. Experience tells us that we receive praise when we exceed someone's expectations, so it's natural for us to start managing those expectations down. In general, we're rewarded when we "under-promise and over-deliver," so we prefer to give only limited promises.

Just as we're concerned about wanting to meet—or even exceed— other people's expectations, we play the same "under-promise" game with ourselves. We don't want to feel inadequate, so we set modest personal goals that can be comfortably attained. Many of us prefer beating a safe goal to falling short of a more aggressive target, so we keep our goals small—but our achievements remain small too.

Now, I'm all for having integrity and upholding our commitments, but under-promising can have negative consequences. Our fear of disappointing ourselves and others can lead us to prioritize avoiding even the risk of underperforming, at the expense of setting more ambitious goals. Our aspirations are constrained by our risk aversion; our desire to exceed expectations directly limits what we believe is possible and seek to achieve in life. Playing it safe often results in lost opportunities.

Pushing Your Thinking

- How do you constrain your ambition by "under-promising and over-delivering"?
- What are your fears about setting and reaching for "stretch" goals?
- Are you *sure* those fears are valid?
- In what situations would you be willing to set a goal outside your safety zone?
- What would it take for you to celebrate falling short of a highly ambitious goal?

Can you get past your past?

*The distinction between the past, present, and future
is only a stubbornly persistent illusion.*
—ALBERT EINSTEIN

I recently watched the movie *Arrival*, a complicated story about non-linear time in which the past, present, and future exist simultaneously. Imagine if you could travel back to the past and affect something that would change your life today. Would you do it? Remember, today's events will be part of your past when tomorrow arrives. How will you remember them and relate to your present once it's become the past?

Our perception of the present is based on the accumulation of past experiences—good and bad—that formed our worldview. Events that affected us, actions by others, and decisions we made, all paired with their respective narratives, are etched in our memories. We carry those memories with us from the past into the future. Some of them serve us well, while others weigh us down with regret. Some people are fond of recounting their stories from the past as the "good old days"—a form of nostalgic romanticism. Others hold onto negative stories from the past for months, years, and even decades, torturing themselves over ancient mistakes and injuries.

While we could debate whether "time heals old wounds," I believe that time does blur the details and facts of the past. That blurring distorts the reality of our memories, often amplifying the negative and muting the positive. So, it's not the actual past we carry as a burden; rather, it's the stories we construct about the past we're holding onto. We developed these narratives, though, and we can change them if we choose. To do this, we need to look at past events from a new perspective—one in which these experiences might have had a silver lining. Finding that silver lining will allow us to reframe the story.

Like any good literary story, life is full of conflicts—Person vs. Person, Person vs. Nature, Person vs. Society, Person vs. Self, and Person vs.

Technology. A friend once told me, "You are the hero of your own story, and it's a great story." Think about it—if you aren't the hero, who is? When we start seeing ourselves as heroes, we can rewrite some of the negative stories of our past and transform them into positive memories. If we can see ourselves as heroes in the present, we might, in time, move past our past.

Pushing Your Thinking

- What story have you been carrying from the past as a burden?
- How can you rewrite that story with a more positive narrative?
- What benefits might you experience by accepting that rewritten story?

Are you lost in the fog of uncertainty?

In this world nothing can be said to be certain,
except death and taxes.
—BENJAMIN FRANKLIN

We wish we lived in a more predictable world, where we knew the outcomes of our decisions ahead of time and could see clearly the path to accomplishment and happiness. Unfortunately, life isn't that simple. Every day we face choices that lead us down different, unknown paths. Many choices present themselves as dilemmas for which there are no obviously right answers. Rather, our decision might offer only a variety of potential consequences, some of which we will not discover until later. Unfortunately, a poor outcome from one decision can easily affect our confidence to make tough choices in the future, even when there were no good options for us to choose from.

Rarely do opportunities present themselves in neon lights with a guaranteed reward. More often, our opportunities are camouflaged as possibilities, with many unknowns to face and challenges to overcome, all in pursuit of some uncertain benefit. Risk-takers thrive on this uncertainty. Whether it's skydiving for the first time or starting a new venture with a business plan on the back of a napkin, some people have the confidence—or audacity—to speculate that their instincts will help them navigate uncertainty. Others see the uncertainty as a fog that obscures possibility, an intimidating cloud that leads them to avoid making decisions or taking action. They see the potential harm in uncertainty—they have the experience to prove it, better to be safe than sorry. When faced with the "fog," they hope that time will clarify their choices, answer their questions, and allow them to reap the benefits of a more informed decision. Sometimes their indecision prevents failure or harm. Most of the time, however, they just never know what could have been.

Pushing Your Thinking

- Do you often find yourself in the fog of uncertainty? Why is that?

- How do you deal with uncertainty? How has that response served you?

- What possibilities might be before you now that you can't see easily?

- What's holding you back from exploring those possibilities?

What would you like to ask IBM Watson?

In 2011, IBM supercomputer Watson emerged victorious on the quiz show *Jeopardy!* from a three-day competition with two of the show's greatest champions, Ken Jennings and Brad Rutter. Watson's victory was the culmination of years of research and development by IBM; Watson can search the equivalent of a million books per second to find the answers.

Since Watson is so "smart," I was hoping it could answer five questions that have stumped me—and others—for some time. So, I decided to send Watson a letter.

Dear Watson,

Congratulations on your success on *Jeopardy!* You clearly have a great deal of intelligence to beat Ken Jennings at the game. I've assembled a list of five questions that have perplexed us humans for a long time, and I'm hoping you can provide some answers.

1. **Why do bad things happen to good people?** We just don't understand. Some of the worst things seem to happen to some of the nicest people. Why isn't life fair?

2. **Why do smart people do stupid things?** We understand when stupid people do stupid things, but what about smart people? Shouldn't they know better?

3. **Do fish see the water they swim in?** After all, we don't see the air we breathe, and most of us don't see or appreciate the culture that surrounds us. Only when the water, air, and culture are diminished do we start to recognize their importance. Why are we so often oblivious to what's all around us?

4. **How many times does a lie need to be repeated before people will believe it as the truth?** Some political figures and commentators knowingly repeat things without any facts, just to

support their ideologies or agendas. Is a lie always a lie or, if we wear people down into believing it, can a lie become a truth?

5. **If life is so short, why do we do so many things we don't like and like so many things we don't do?** Many things seem important, but few really matter to our happiness. Why are we preoccupied with activities that provide such a short-lived sense of satisfaction? Why are we satisfied with just the hope that we might eventually get to the meaningful things that will make us happy, rather than making the time for them?

Watson, I understand that you are busy—I hope, working to end world hunger and stop global warming—but any insight you have on these questions would be appreciated.

Yours truly,

Glenn Mangurian
Human Being
Hingham, MA 02043

Pushing Your Thinking

- If Watson can't answer these questions, who can?
- Do you have any answers?
- What questions would you like to ask Watson?

Can you handle the truth?

There is a famous courtroom scene in the movie *A Few Good Men* between Tom Cruise, an inexperienced Navy JAG, and Jack Nicholson, the testifying commanding officer:

TOM CRUISE [SHOUTS]: Did you order the "Code Red"?!!

JACK NICHOLSON [SHOUTS BACK]: You want answers?

TOM CRUISE: I think I'm entitled to them.

JACK NICHOLSON: You want answers?

TOM CRUISE: I want the truth!

JACK NICHOLSON: You can't handle the truth!

Most of us want to hear the truth—as long as it's favorable. When I was a child, my grandmother would tell me, "If you don't have something nice to say, don't say it." She called it "being polite." Little did I know then that "being polite" was common adult behavior.

To be polite, many people withhold how they feel or what they think to avoid offending and creating conflict. Most of us prefer to avoid conflict—disagreement and contention are often mistaken for disrespect. It's easier to talk behind someone's back than to communicate directly and honestly, and straight talk is not usually intended for public consumption. But two people can easily have different perspectives on the same situation. If I'm afraid that voicing my truth will compete with your truth, will either of us be willing to speak plainly?

Occasionally, there is sufficient mutual trust and respect for both people to lay their cards on the table. This kind of straight talk only occurs when it's mutually beneficial. Unconsciously, we all ask ourselves, "Do the benefits of talking straight and working through a conflict exceed the potential costs in terms of personal risk and damaged relationships?" That tradeoff is not usually easy to assess.

Speaking tough truths is hard enough with our peers, but it poses different challenges when there's a power imbalance in the relationship.

In one of my Uncommon Leadership seminars, I interviewed former presidential advisor David Gergen. I asked him, "How does one advise the leader of the free world?" He responded:

> Carefully! In terms of talking to presidents, the first thing to learn is to speak truth to power. Sometimes you can be out of step with what the president wants to hear, and you risk disfavor. It is probably even more important to speak conscience to power.

If our friends and colleagues aren't comfortable being straight with us, what possibilities for improvement might we be missing?

Pushing Your Thinking

- Whom do you rely on to tell you the truth? Do you usually receive it well?

- Do you encourage direct and honest communication even when it might result in contention? If so, how?

- Who relies on you for straight talk? Do you provide it? Are they able to hear you?

Do we expect our leaders to inspire us?

Do you care what our leaders say or how they say it? Do you look for competence or inspiration in your leaders? Obviously you're not willing to follow incompetent leaders, but are you necessarily going to follow the most competent? You might, but without the enthusiasm you'd have for a leader who taps into your passions.

MOTIVATION VS. INSPIRATION. Many people use the terms *motivation* and *inspiration* interchangeably, but do they really mean the same thing? Not quite. Motivation is external, the reason that we decide to act or try to achieve a goal, a tangible reward. Inspiration, on the other hand, is something that evokes a strong emotional response in us. It taps into our soul, drawing on our sense of purpose and our deep need for personal fulfillment.

FOUR QUESTIONS. Author and speaker Simon Sinek often talks about the subject of inspiration. He asserts that "People aren't inspired by what you do; people are inspired by why you do it."[13] We enthusiastically follow exceptional leaders not because we have to, but because we want to. We're inspired by the "why" of what they do and less by the "what" or the "how." We're moved to follow leaders who tap into our passions, not for them, but for ourselves. Their leadership reinforces and validates our values, demonstrating their importance to others. As we decide which leaders to follow, we seek answers to four questions:

1. Do I know your beliefs and values?
2. Do I know why you believe what you believe?
3. Do I see your behavior as consistent with your values?"
4. Do your beliefs resonate with my beliefs, and are they sourced from the same values?

"I BELIEVE ..." In 1963, 250,000 people showed up on the mall in Washington, DC, to hear Dr. Martin Luther King, Jr. speak. There was no Twitter to get the word out and no Facebook page of followers, yet a quarter million people showed up at the right time on the right day to listen to Dr. King. Here is how Sinek describes King's ability to inspire:

> He didn't go around telling people what needed to change in America. He went around and told people what he believed. "I believe, I believe, I believe." And people who believed what he believed took his cause, and they made it their own, and they told other people. How many of them showed up for him? Zero. They showed up for themselves. It's what they believed about America that got them to travel in a bus for eight hours to stand in the sun in Washington in the middle of August. We followed, not for him, but for ourselves.[14]

Pushing Your Thinking

- Who in your circle of friends, relatives, or colleagues inspires you? Do they know it?

- How are you affected by their leadership? What possibilities does their leadership create?

- Who is inspired by you? What do they see in you that inspires them?

- How would you like them to be affected by your leadership? What possibilities does your leadership create for them?

Pushing the Edge of Action

The previous sections examined how our experiences influence our thinking and our thinking shapes our awareness of possibilities. When we see the world as full of possibilities, we are more likely to take action. We may act in our own self-interest, or selflessly on behalf of others, but we're able to make that decision because we recognize the potential for success.

Acting to realize possibilities is not always easy. In some instances, we may be reluctant to act because of the uncertainty of the outcome. In other cases, we may be fearful of potential unintended consequences. We may not have the necessary self-confidence to accept the responsibility of our actions.

This section poses questions and offers insights that can help you translate possibilities into opportunities. Acting on the opportunities allows you to realize new successes. It is up to you—it's a choice within your control. Good luck pushing the edge.

Are you authentic?

Be yourself. Everyone else is already taken.
—OSCAR WILDE

What is authenticity? The simple answer is that we know it when we see it—and we don't see it often. Authentic people are often described as being genuine, sincere, and self-aware. We recognize them as having integrity and consistently adhering to their values.

Authenticity isn't something we do or say; it comes from deep inside us. Authenticity is an intimate expression of who we are; it's *our soul in action*. It's also largely defined by how others experience us. To be authentic, we need to be transparent, allowing others to understand our core values and then evaluate our actions for consistency. Transparency requires vulnerability—something few of us are comfortable with. It requires finding a balance between preserving our privacy and opening ourselves up to public scrutiny.

For example, in my graduate leadership course, I have students identify a person in their lives whom they regard as authentic. They then compose a personal note acknowledging the person's authenticity—not a memo or an email, but a handwritten note. Although they're not required to send the message, I encourage them to share their admiration with the person they're acknowledging.

The students have no difficulty identifying an authentic person in their lives. They all write heartfelt notes for the assignment, but few are comfortable sharing their messages with the individuals who've touched them. Some feel embarrassed, while others are concerned about how the person may react. A few recount receiving and saving a similar thoughtful note, and they relate how they never forgot the gift of positive expression. They were unaware of how their seemingly natural actions had such a profound effect on someone else. For many of us, though, acknowledging authenticity is an uncomfortable or unnatural act. We are conditioned to keep our emotions to ourselves, and we shy away from "straight talk," even when it's positive.

What a missed opportunity for an honest expression of appreciation—an authentic act of recognition.

Think of people you know whom you consider to be authentic. They probably don't know how their authenticity affects you. Look for an opportunity to tell them.

Pushing Your Thinking

- We seldom think about our own authenticity. Do others experience you as authentic?

- If so, how do you know? How does your authenticity affect those around you?

- If not, what is in the way?

- How might those around you relate to you differently if you removed the barriers to your authenticity?

What do you say when you don't know what to say?

If you're like me, you've probably had the experience of something bad happening to a friend and not knowing what to say. Rather than risk saying an inappropriate thing, we often default to something worse—we say nothing at all. We try to think of an empathetic response, but the fear of putting our foot in our mouth can lead us to avoid the situation altogether. Saying nothing, however, can leave our friends and loved ones feeling isolated in their grief.

Few of us are good at coping with grief—we can't practice the feeling of loss ahead of time. In the movies, everyone knows what to say in response to a personal tragedy. In real life, however, we often feel perplexed and inadequate. Our hearts want to be with our friends and share with them in their time of sorrow, but our heads lack the words to express our regrets.

I'm certain that scores of well-intentioned people have said to a grieving friend, "God doesn't give you any more than you can handle." That statement implies that the person has been selected to suffer because of the belief that he or she can deal with the situation effectively. Statements of this sort don't really mean much to the person who is suffering.[15, 16]

Before you express anything, put yourself in your friend's shoes. Don't say, "I know just how you feel," because you can't know another person's grief, even if you've been through a significant loss yourself. Many times, words are less important than our willingness to just be present and listen. Resist the temptation to make up answers to the inevitable question "why?" Unless you truly know, you can't really make sense of an incomprehensible situation.

Be creative with ways to stay in touch. When you say, "Let me know when I can help," most people won't know how to ask for your help. They may fear that your offer of assistance was simple courtesy, and that you don't actually expect to be called on. If you're serious, you might make suggestions for concrete ways you can help, such as cooking a meal, driving a child to and from school, or assisting in grocery shopping.

When you're struggling to find the right words to say, remember—a simple, silent touch can mean more than 1,000 words, and a hug is worth 1,000 touches.

Pushing Your Thinking

- Reflect on a time when something bad happened to a friend. Did you struggle with what to say?

- Reflect on a time when something bad happened to you. What was most comforting to you?

- Who in your life might be struggling right now? What might you do to help comfort the person?

Do you accept invitations to arguments?

Remember the days when you would receive a snail mail invitation to a special event with instructions on how to respond? The only formal invitations we seem to get these days are to weddings—other invitations tend to come in the form of evites. That word didn't even exist 15 years ago, and now you can respond online and even view the guest list from home! But no matter how they arrive, we look forward to invitations to celebrate with family and friends. Sadly, not all invitations are for happy gatherings.

Sometimes in life we encounter statements that seem to be "invitations" to argue, openings for disagreement and contention. These invitations rarely come via the snail mail—they usually arrive in person, in an email, or on social media. Most of the time, the invitation to an argument is subtle and disguised as an opinion. Someone says something you don't like or you don't agree with. You may even interpret the statement as a criticism or personal attack. Maybe you've had one of your buttons pushed and are employing a knee-jerk reaction.

You don't have to accept these invitations to arguments, though. You can reject them—"return to sender, addressee unwilling to accept"—and practice letting go of your need to be right. Alternatively, you can respond with *jujutsu*, a Japanese art of gentle, soft, supple, flexible engagement. Rather than responding to the invitation and confronting the "attacker," you might say, "That's an interesting point. Why do you believe that?" Another possibility is to pivot to a related subject that's less charged, subtly directing everyone's energy away from the disagreement.

Just because someone invites you to argue doesn't mean you have to accept—you have choices. The key is to install a "circuit breaker" in your brain so when one of your buttons is pushed, you don't immediately react. This pause gives you the opportunity to decide if you'll ignore or reject the invitation.

A bit of humor can help defuse the situation, too. So the next time you are cordially invited to an argument ask "Is it black-tie optional?"

Pushing Your Thinking

- Do you notice when you're invited to an argument? How do those invitations usually arrive?

- What can you do to interrupt your knee-jerk response?

- What responses can you practice to help you resist the temptation to engage in arguments?

Why do smart people do stupid things?

Many people we admire, whether they're public figures or even friends and colleagues, have done some pretty stupid things—actions that don't make sense and have predictable negative consequences. Why do these seemingly smart people do or say such stupid things? Shouldn't they know better? Most of us just scratch our heads and wonder, but I think there are three possible explanations:

THEY BELIEVE THEY CAN GET AWAY WITH IT. Many smart people are confident, and that confidence occasionally crosses the line into arrogance. Some people lose touch with reality and start living in their own world—a world in which they're smart enough to get away with anything. They're often intoxicated by their perceived power and believe that no one will find out about their mistakes.

THEY THINK THEIR STUPID ACTIONS ARE SMART. Smart people, when challenged over their actions, often express their opinion that the rest of the world is stupid, and they are actually the smart ones. Some seemingly intelligent people react negatively when they see their ideas and opinions challenged or rejected. They're really smart, so how could they be wrong? These people get swept up in the narrative of their own importance and have convinced themselves they're incapable of making any serious errors or misjudgments.

THEY ARE NOT AS SMART AS WE—OR THEY—THINK. We all have different definitions of the term *smart*—clever, intelligent, shrewd, powerful, successful—but as computer scientist Alan Kay once said, "Perspective is worth 80 IQ points."[17] When we lose our perspective, we are apt to do stupid things. Perspective is what keeps us grounded; it allows us to see the bigger picture and to respect others' opinions. People who've lost their perspective lack a critical dimension of intelligence.

We all, on occasion, do things we later regret—that's called being human. Ideally, we learn from our mistakes and make amends. For some people, though, it's impossible to admit mistakes, let alone apologize. I call that being stupid!

Pushing Your Thinking

- Recall a situation from the past in which you later regretted your actions. What prompted you to act in the first place?
- What, if anything, did you do to recover or learn from your decision?
- How can we be sure we're making smart choices?
- How can we teach children to think about the consequences of their choices?

Why are transitions so difficult?

Years ago I read *Passages*, the best-selling book by Gail Sheehy.[18] It's based on the 1978 work of Daniel Levinson, *The Seasons of a Man's Life*.[19] Both books taught me that transitions are part of life and that anxiety is a part of transitions.

I recently made the transition from "baby boomer" to "senior citizen baby boomer." I became eligible for Medicare. How can it be that a baby boomer is now eligible for senior discounts at the movies? I'm not sure I like it, but isn't that the way it goes with transitions? Some transitions, like aging, are beyond our control. Others, like changing jobs or moving, we undertake by choice. Either way, most of them are extraordinarily difficult—but why?

A transition involves moving from the known to the unknown. It's the process of leaving the past and accepting an uncertain future. Transitions are about endings and new beginnings. I have an expression about transition: "I am no longer who I was and not yet who I am becoming. I am a work in progress."

We're all works in progress. It's not that transitions are inherently difficult, although many are. Our fear of the unknown can trigger our anxiety. We can easily develop negative stories about what the transition could bring. Even if we think we know what's coming in a transition, we can't be certain, and leaving behind the familiar is difficult.

So for me, it's time to create a pleasant story about my new age status. I think I'll make mine an adventure story. How will you write your transition stories?

Pushing Your Thinking

- Think back over past transitions that were enjoyable and relatively easy. What made them pleasant and straightforward?
- How about the difficult transitions? What made them difficult? How did you move through those transitions?
- What current transition are you in or approaching? What can you learn from your past transitions and apply today?

Do you make it a great day?

The tragedy of life is not that it ends so soon,
but that we wait so long to begin it.

—W. M. LEWIS
President of George Washington University and Lafayette College

A few years ago, my daughter Laura and her husband returned to Massachusetts after two years living in Fairbanks, Alaska. Upon her return, I noticed that when I talked to Laura, she'd end each conversation with the expression, "Make it a great day." I'd usually respond, "You have a great day too." The other day we went through this "make it a great day" routine, but Laura replied, "Don't have a great day, Dad. Make it great."

Have a great day. Make it a great day. What's the difference? I finally got it. We have direct influence over much of what happens in our lives, and complete control over how we relate to events. One phrase illustrates the power we have over our circumstances, while the other implies our circumstances have power over us. We can do what we must to get through the day, or we can choose to make the day count. Sometimes great days happen, but most of the time great days are great because we make them so—something we don't do often enough. And if we wait for others to make our days great, we'll end up waiting a long time.

Each day we have the opportunity to enrich our lives and the lives of those around us. The best place to start is by practicing gratitude for the abundance in our lives. We can be thankful for the experiences we've had, the people we've met, and the lessons we've learned. Then we should look for ways to make a difference—in our work, in our family, with our friends, or with perfect strangers. Simple actions such as opening a door, saying "thank you," and even just smiling are acts of generosity. We can make the world better one person at a time.

To make today great, grab a happy attitude, look for opportunities to laugh, and don't take yourself too seriously. Instead, choose to have a little fun—without the guilt. How we relate to the circumstances in our lives is a choice. It all starts today, so make it great—or not. It's up to you.

Pushing Your Thinking

- Are your days generally great or not so great?
- Do you actively work to make your days great, or do you accept each day as it comes?
- What can you do, starting today, to make your days great?

Why is it so hard to say, "I'm sorry"?

Never ruin an apology with an excuse.
—BENJAMIN FRANKLIN

We are human and we make mistakes, intentional or not. Sometimes those mistakes adversely affect others. In those situations we can easily feel embarrassed. Some of us will try to hide from our mistakes or shift the blame to someone else. The appropriate response is to own the mistake and offer an authentic apology to those who may have been hurt. Taking responsibility for our mistakes and saying, "I'm sorry" can make us feel vulnerable, but it can also liberate us from carrying the burden of the error into the future.

What exactly do we mean when we say, "I'm sorry"? The statement can mean many things. "I'm sorry" may be an apology—"I didn't mean to hurt you," a regret—"I should not have done that," or even an expression of empathy—"I empathize with your pain, suffering, or situation." Sometimes "I'm sorry" is offered as an excuse when we're wrong, in an attempt to lessen the consequences. I'm sure that you have experienced someone saying, "I'm sorry" and sensed that the person didn't really mean it. For example, "Hey, I said I'm sorry—now get over it."

University of Pennsylvania professor Maurice Schweitzer[20] believes that people are afraid to apologize for two reasons: "One is loss of status. The other is that apologizing makes you more vulnerable." And yet apologies are "incredibly powerful in terms of rebuilding a relationship," Schweitzer says. "They help people move beyond an error. They restore a sense of rapport among the parties involved." An authentic "I'm sorry" can not only repair a strained or broken relationship but also deepen the relationship. It signals to the hurt person that you care enough about the relationship to admit the mistake, acknowledge the adverse effects, and apologize.

The digital age has brought us apology websites. It's never been easier than with an e-pology. As for me, I prefer the old-fashioned approach—a face-to-face, direct, and authentic, "I'm sorry."

Pushing Your Thinking

- Can you distinguish an authentic "I'm sorry" from an insincere one?

- When you discover you're wrong, do you offer a genuine apology?

- How do you feel after you say, "I'm sorry"?

Are you proud of
being different?

Business Strategy 101 teaches us to differentiate companies from their competitors, since imitation places a company in a crowded pack where price is the primary basis of competition. Some think that Society 101 teaches people to do the opposite—to conform. Of course, we need to conform to some forms of social etiquette, but imitation puts us in another crowded pack—one in which we run the risk of denying what's uniquely special about us as individuals.

In the early 20th century, the term *melting pot*[21] was a metaphor used to describe the "blending," or assimilation, of immigrants into a new society. In the 1970s, the melting pot model was challenged by the theory of multiculturalism. Proponents of multiculturalism asserted that cultural differences within society are valuable and should be preserved, proposing an alternative metaphor of a mosaic. Today, most believe that pluralism[22] makes our country special. Pluralism is the belief that there should be diverse and competing centers of power in society, allowing ideas and innovation to flourish. It's a fundamental tenet of our culture and worldview, and the philosophy that has helped our country attract the best minds from around the world.

Steve Jobs, the American son of a Syrian immigrant, was widely regarded as a master innovator and pioneer. He was respected for creating products we didn't know we needed. Jobs told us to "think different"[23] or, as others might say, to think "outside the box." But more important, Jobs encouraged us not just to think different but to be different. The first step is realizing who you are and what makes you different. Unfortunately, many people experience ridicule, teasing, and social alienation because of their differences. When youth or adults are bullied for their differences, peer attacks can undermine their self-confidence and prevent them from believing in themselves.

Here is what Steve Jobs famously said about being different.

> Here's to the Crazy Ones. The misfits. The rebels. The trouble-makers. The round pegs in the square holes. The ones who see things differently. They're not fond of rules, and they have no respect for the status quo.
>
> You can quote them, disagree with them, glorify, or vilify them. About the only thing you can't do is ignore them. Because they change things. They push the human race forward. And while some may see them as the crazy ones, we see genius. Because the people who are crazy enough to think they can change the world are the ones who *do*![24]

I'm different from anyone else in the world and proud of it. Imagine a world where we're all the same—how boring! Now, imagine a world where we celebrate our differences. How might respect for our differences reveal new opportunities and lead to coordinated action?

Pushing Your Thinking

- What differences make you special? When did you realize your uniqueness?
- What is special about your friends and professional colleagues?
- What is special about your children? Do they know it?
- How do we encourage people to feel confident about who they are?

Do you know how to "just smile"?

The people from the Northeast have a reputation for being fast-paced and preoccupied with getting from here to there. They often walk with their minds multiprocessing and seldom pause to offer a "good morning." I used to be one of those people.

I'll never forget an experience I had 16 years ago. I had recently returned home from my two-month stay in the hospital recovering from a spinal cord injury. I was out in public for the first time. As I rolled along the sidewalk in downtown Hingham, I noticed that everyone looked away as I approached them in my wheelchair. It was like making eye contact would somehow embarrass or injure me. Was I so fragile that people needed to look elsewhere?

I decided to try something new the next time I went out in public. As I approached people, I'd look them in the eye and smile. No words, just a smile. The result was surprising. Passersby smiled back and maintained eye contact. Some even said, "Good morning!" or "Good afternoon!" Think about it—two strangers smiling and making eye contact in New England—what a novel experience! I've continued my practice of smiling with consistent results. My able-bodied wife even tried it, and sure enough, if you direct a smile to someone, the person will usually smile back.

I did a little research on smiling. Smiling is something that's understood across cultures, races, religions, and genders. It's internationally recognized as a welcoming signal of self-confidence and happiness. When someone smiles, the person become likable and approachable. People who smile can produce a positive effect on others, which correlates with greater trust. Think about times when you're stressed or upset. If someone were to smile at you, wouldn't you start to feel a little better? All from a simple smile. If everyone smiled more, the world would be a friendlier place. Give it a try. You might be surprised by the response.

Pushing Your Thinking

- While walking, are you preoccupied thinking?
- Do you smile a lot or greet friends and colleagues with a "good morning"?
- Do you notice when people look you in the eye and smile? Do you smile back?

Do people hear what you mean?

Do you ever find yourself misunderstood? Do people hear something you didn't intend to say? My guess is that misunderstandings happen more often than you think, because we are constantly communicating messages beyond our words. In fact, our words constitute only a small fraction of how our messages will be received; the silent signals we send will either reinforce or undermine them. A lack of additional, nonverbal cues is one of the reasons memos and emails are especially likely to be misinterpreted.

Albert Mehrabian, Professor Emeritus of Psychology at UCLA, is known for his research on the relative importance of verbal and nonverbal messages. His findings on the inconsistency between our intended messages and the way they're actually received is known as the 7-38-55 rule.[25]

According to Mehrabian, three elements of communication account for our interpretation of—and emotional response to—what we hear. He reports that words account for 7 percent of our overall feelings about a message, tone of voice accounts for 38 percent, and body language accounts for 55 percent. The percentages seem overly precise to me, but that's his research. These nonverbal messages are communicated via the speed and rhythm of our speech, through our tone, gestures, and postures, as well as by our facial and vocal expressions—and they all outweigh our words in determining how an audience feels about our message.

These nonverbal elements of communication are particularly important when a speaker's feelings are incongruent with the person's words. When words conflict with the tone of voice or nonverbal cues, people tend to believe the tonality and nonverbal behavior above the words. If facial expressions or body language is inconsistent with the verbal message, the feelings conveyed by the body will dominate and determine the message's overall impact. If the words are positive but the tone or body language appears negative, the message will be experienced negatively.

Remember, though, in addition to Mehrabian's 7-38-55 rule of verbal and nonverbal communication, the story we have about the messenger will also determine what we hear. This story, which forms the filter through which we process the communication, is extraordinarily powerful. If we hold the messenger in a negative light, we'll almost certainly hear his or her message negatively, regardless of what was said or how it was said.

Pushing Your Thinking

- Think of a recent communication that someone misinterpreted. Was it your words, your tone of voice, your body language that caused your message to be misinterpreted?

- What was going on in your background that may have caused your communication intent to be interpreted differently?

- Think of a person you don't particularly like. When was the last time you heard that person communicate something that created a positive feeling with you?

Are you a David or a Goliath?

The original story of David and Goliath is biblical, with a young underdog, David, and a giant warrior, Goliath, confronting each other—Goliath with his armor and shield, David with his staff and sling. David hurls a stone from his sling and hits Goliath in the center of his forehead, killing him and proving that the little guy can beat the odds.

Best-selling author Malcolm Gladwell has written a book titled *David and Goliath*.[26] The overarching thesis of Gladwell's David and Goliath is that for the strong, "the same qualities that appear to give them strength are often the sources of great weakness," whereas for the weak, "the act of facing overwhelming odds produces greatness and beauty." Gladwell calls this "the theory of desirable difficulty." Gladwell gives several examples of people who achieved greatness not by luck, skill, or training, but rather through successful overcompensation for a major weakness. Gladwell asserts that hard work to overcome a fundamental personal limitation can create an against-all-odds triumph.

Gladwell gives examples of superstars who have achieved success despite their acknowledged learning constraints. One of his prominent examples is David Boies, the super-lawyer, who has been involved in various high-profile cases, including representing Vice President Al Gore in *Bush v. Gore*. Boies who has dyslexia didn't learn to read until the third grade. Gladwell recounts how Boies's mother would read stories to him when he was a child and Boies would memorize them because he couldn't follow the words on the page. Boies asserts that his dyslexia forced him to compensate by developing skills of observation and memory, which he used to excel in law school and further exploited in the courtroom.

Here is my interpretation of Gladwell's theory of desirable difficulty: some people are primarily driven by the fear that they will be trapped by some fundamental personal weakness. Harnessing that fear, channeling that energy, can lead to extraordinary results. Working to compensate for our limitations by developing critical strengths will allow us to find success. Gladwell believes we can all be "Davids" if we embrace our limitations as a pathway to success. Interesting idea. Does it resonate with you?

Pushing Your Thinking

- Do you know someone who has achieved success by overcompensating for a limitation or constraint?
- Do you know someone who has failed by misusing a personal strength?
- Do you have a disadvantage that makes you stronger?

Are you haunted by "woulda, coulda, shouldas"?

We all have regrets—a decision we made or didn't make, something we said or did that we'd like to change. Some of us are always second-guessing ourselves; we feel sorry, disappointed, or distressed about things we wish would, could, or should be different. Many times, our "woulda, coulda, shoulda" reflects a missed opportunity, a risk we didn't take.

These regrets can easily devolve into a vicious cycle. The more we fret about something, the worse it seems to get. Yet no matter how much we agonize over our past actions and decisions, they remain unchangeable—what's in the past is in the past. At some point, we need to let go and move on. Often that's easier said than done.

You probably know someone who continues to second-guess decisions he or she made years ago. Some people carry regrets around for a lifetime, suffering from lack of confidence and beating themselves up over simple mistakes. Some of these individuals are perfectionists, people who are never satisfied with themselves and live in a perpetual state of unhappiness.

Today many of us get caught up with our to-do lists and neglect "doing" the things that are meaningful to us. Every now and then, we need to interrupt our daily routines to make time for things that bring us enjoyment. Start with an hour a week and grow it from there. You might replace regrets with a little more happiness.

Don't let the present pass with woulda, coulda, shouldas. Discover a worthwhile "did" that you can do today.

Pushing Your Thinking

- Do you carry regrets from the past?
- What can you do to release those regrets?
- What can you do today to prevent tomorrow's woulda, coulda, shouldas?

Do you tend toward "doing the right thing" or "doing things right"?

We are often faced with dilemmas in which we seek to do the right thing but the right thing is sometimes not obvious. In other situations, people expect us to fulfill our obligations through flawless execution. Do we value both equally? My experience tells me that people tend toward one or the other, often without knowing it.

DOING THINGS RIGHT. In today's world, not only do we expect people to fulfill their commitments; we also want them to do things right, performing as planned or instructed in order to achieve the desired result. Workers are recognized and rewarded for consistently doing their jobs right. These dependable performers are difficult to find; they're quickly snatched up by good leaders who recognize their value as team members. Wouldn't each of us love to have a go-to person we could always count on to get things done?

DOING THE RIGHT THING. Many situations require us to exercise our judgment, sometimes spontaneously in the moment. What seemed like the right approach at the beginning may have proven inappropriate and led to unintended results, requiring us to adjust our strategy. Circumstances may have changed since the instructions were given, or the assignment may have been flawed from the start. Maybe it wasn't thought through and doesn't make sense, or maybe it even violates a personal value or ethical boundary. When that happens, we hope people will decide against "doing things right" and do the right thing instead.

THE "RIGHT" DILEMMA. Over time we start to lean toward a particular version of "right." Our past experience of rewards and consequences has taught us to act in a certain way, to prioritize one action over another. Those who focus on execution excellence may end up suppressing their own judgment—in business, after all, employees are sometimes asked to do things they don't understand. As we assume increased responsibilities, we'll need to use our own judgment more and more. We'll need to be prepared to deviate from our instructions and improvise solutions when necessary, while still achieving the desired result.

Pushing Your Thinking

- Do those who take instructions from you know when to do what is right, even if it deviates from your instructions? How can you make sure they know?

- Do you know when to do what is right and not necessarily what you were asked to do? On what basis do you make your decision?

- How might we teach children to both follow instructions and exercise their own judgment?

What's the truth about lying?

Are people lying more, or are more people getting caught? Maybe it's both. The fact is, everybody lies for some reason.[27] In many cases, it feels easier for us to lie than to tell the truth. When I think about why we lie, I come up with five motivations:

TO AVOID CONFLICT. For adults, courtesy often is preferred over direct and honest communication. People politely withhold how they feel or what they think for fear of offending someone and creating conflict. Disagreement and contention are often mistaken for disrespect, so we lie to avoid them.

TO CONCEAL A WEAKNESS. Recognizing our flaws is not easy, but admitting them to others is significantly more difficult. Exposing our weaknesses to others makes us feel vulnerable and insecure; lying may allow us to save face or look good.

TO GET AHEAD. Sometimes people lie for personal gain. In these cases, we think—or hope—we can get away with a lie and advance ourselves. If we succeed, we may even become habitual liars. Habitual liars see lying as a perfectly acceptable strategy in the game of life, lying whenever it will benefit them to do so.

TO INFLUENCE OTHERS. Some people make promises they can't keep in order to persuade people. They may speak half-truths to sway others to their way of thinking, or they may lie in the hope of obtaining acceptance by telling someone what they think they want to hear. These lies often stem from either low self-esteem or the need for control.

TO BELIEVE WE ARE RIGHT. Sometimes our lies don't even involve others; self-deception is how we lie to ourselves. We like to think we're always right—that we know the truth and always do the right thing—so when evidence suggests otherwise, a lie might be the quickest way to reassure ourselves. We lie and tell ourselves that we're right when we can't face that we're wrong.

We dislike being lied to because lies break trust. When a person lies, that person has broken the unspoken expectation of mutual integrity. If you lie to me once, how do I know when I should believe you? Since the issue of trust is on the line, coming clean about a lie as soon as possible is the best way to mend fences. Unfortunately, many people lie about the lie, doubling down on their deception.

So if many lie, how do we overcome the temptation to lie to others? Most of us believe that people are inherently well meaning, especially our friends and family. We rely on their trust and honesty to cope with life's challenges.

Pushing Your Thinking

- Do you remember the last time you lied and got away with it? How did you feel?

- When was the last time you lied and got caught? How did you feel?

- When was the last time you told the truth and created conflict? If conflict was not your intent, what was it about how you communicated the truth that created the conflict?

- How do you regain the trust of someone you have lied to?

- What does it take for you to forgive someone who has lied to you?

Do you have the touch?

People won't care how much you know
until they know how much you care.
—THEODORE ROOSEVELT

A touch can be a way of showing comfort and compassion during a time of hardship, adversity, or personal crisis. I'm talking about a simple touch to the hand or arm during a difficult situation to show you care. Some people know when a touch is needed and how to deliver it, but others fear their touch may be interpreted as an invasion of personal space.

CARING BEYOND THE CARE. I've had my share of hospital stays. At times, our medical system can feel more like a factory than a healing institution. While all my doctors and nurses offered words of encouragement, some offered additional comfort and caring through touch. I noticed that most nurses had that special touch, but most doctors kept their distance. I doubt that touch is taught in medical or nursing school, but it should be. The touch is a way to add compassion and humanity to an otherwise impersonal healthcare system.

A TOUCH IS WORTH 1,000 WORDS. The benefit of touching is not limited to hospital situations. During any hardship, adversity, or personal crisis, a touch can be a way of providing comfort. The touch is not merely physical contact; it is also a nonverbal, authentic expression of caring. Given at the right time, with the right intention, and with mutual eye contact, a touch can demonstrate empathy and amplify words of support and encouragement.

A HUG IS WORTH 1,000 TOUCHES. Did you ever notice how often little children hug each other? I noticed that even my adult children greet their friends with a hug rather than a handshake. A hug can be a demonstration of emotional warmth, arising from the joy at meeting someone or an indication of support, comfort, and consolation. A silent hug and smile speak volumes. Hugging is healthy for the body and the soul. Most people love a hug. Remember, the person who is the hardest to hug is usually the one who needs it the most.

Now, I'm not advocating you go around hugging everyone you meet—although that might be an interesting practice. Instead, look for opportunities to say "hello" and "thank you" with a hug. You may be surprised at the difference it makes.

Pushing Your Thinking

- Do you remember the last time someone gave you the touch? How did it make you feel?

- Do you have the touch?

- Think of someone you know who could use a touch or a hug. Give it. How did it make the person feel? How did it make you feel?

What kind of leader are you?

Everyone plays a leadership role in some aspect of their lives, whether it's in their career, community, or family. I recently read a blog post by Dr. Manfred F. R. Kets de Vries, the Distinguished Professor of Leadership Development and Organizational Change at INSEAD in France. His post was titled "The Eight Archetypes of Leadership."[28] It got me thinking about my consulting experience and the recurring patterns of leadership I observed through my everyday experiences. Here is my expanded list of leadership types:

- **ARCHITECTS** take a vision and translate it into a design for action.

- **BUILDERS** take something new and make it bigger and better.

- **CATALYSTS** are drawn to "messy" and challenging situations. They are masters at effecting change.

- **CHESS MASTERS** are capable of thinking five steps ahead. They anticipate changes in their surroundings and envision future scenarios before they become problems.

- **COACHES** know how to get the best out of people. They empower and encourage the people around them to achieve their goals.

- **DEAL MAKERS** are great at bringing people together. They are skilled at creating win–win situations, and they thrive on negotiation.

- **DREAMERS** imagine creating things that don't exist. They are innovators, unconstrained by the practical, and they attract others who believe in making the impossible possible.

- **EXECUTORS** know how to get difficult and ambitious things done. They maintain focus, are persistent, overcome challenges, and follow through on their commitments.

- **INNOVATORS** are focused on making something new—or making the current situation better. They have a discomfort with the status quo and are not deterred by failure or constrained by a narrow worldview.

- **MOTIVATORS** inspire others to believe in themselves and take action. They are skilled at understanding what people need in order to perform at their best and work to help them attain their goals.

- **OPERATORS** strive to have everything run smoothly, like a "well-oiled machine." They are effective at setting up the structures and systems needed to meet objectives.

- **ORCHESTRATORS** are great influencers, often without full authority over others. They are skilled at coalescing teams of diverse individuals aligned around a common purpose.

- **STRATEGISTS** are skilled at sensing and adapting to changes in their surroundings. They provide vision, strategic direction, and creative thinking.

Of course, no one possesses all of these skills; we're all a combination of several of these types. We're most effective as leaders when we can appropriately match our specific leadership skills to the current circumstances.

Pushing Your Thinking

- What types of leadership do you identify with?

- Would your friends and colleagues see you the same way?

- What can you learn from the way others experience you as a leader?

Can you realize what's possible?

Possibilities abound, but we must first teach ourselves to see what's possible—only then can we appreciate a possibility as a reality. Every day, seemingly impossible challenges become possible achievements for someone.

On May 26, 2001, I suffered an unprovoked disc rupture that pressed against my spinal cord, leaving the lower half of my body permanently paralyzed. Life, as I knew it, was over. I had a choice: wallow in the why and feel sorry for myself, or create a new life. For me, it was not much of a choice—who wants to waste his or her life stuck in a state of wallow?

WE ALL ENCOUNTER ADVERSITY IN OUR LIVES. It's a cliché to say that what doesn't kill you makes you stronger, but most people can accept that idea as generally true. Since my injury, I've had the opportunity to engage in numerous conversations with people who've been through life-altering events. I've discovered that everyone will face at least one of four types of adversity in their lives—professional, financial, medical, or interpersonal—and most will carry the burden silently. My adversity is visual. In fact, my paralysis is confrontational—in a group, I "stand" out.

LOSS AMPLIFIES WHAT REMAINS. As I wrote this book, I reflected on how my life has changed since that day. Becoming paralyzed is without question the worst thing that's ever happened to me. Life is a constant struggle. Yet, the experience has allowed me to take stock of what I have and cut through the clutter of daily life. Rather than being preoccupied with what I can't do, I focus on the things I can do. New doors have opened that I never could have foreseen. I'm as active as ever—I teach, write, speak, and serve on several boards. My loss has also provided me with a new perspective on life.

MANY THINGS ARE IMPORTANT, BUT FEW THINGS REALLY MATTER. Do you know what really matters to you? If you're like me, you make to-do lists. While those lists are important for getting things done, most of the items don't really matter. What matters most to me is my family. Since my injury, I've seen my son, Mark, and daughter, Laura, become vibrant adults. My wife, Gail, is my hero and inspiration, and we are proud grandparents. Without her, I know I would not be writing this book.

CHOOSE TO GO FORWARD. Accepting adversity and moving on isn't easy—it can take time. You don't have to like or try to justify what's happened. You just need to decide you can live with it. After all, your happiness is more important than righting the injustices of the past. I've learned that we actually control very little in life, but the choices we make *are* within our control. No one can take away that capability. We can choose to go forward.

BOUNCE BACK. I had an active life and fulfilling career prior to my injury. It was a wonderful life. I call that life, "Glenn 1.0." It became the foundation for my life today. Many of us underestimate our ability to withstand adversity. We don't realize how much we're capable of doing and achieving. People won't remember how far we fall but rather how high we bounce back.

My new life, "Glenn 2.0," is a work in progress. I'm no longer who I was, and I'm not yet who I'm becoming. Yet I know that this life is full of new adventures. I may experience them sitting down, but in a way, I am standing taller than ever.

Notes

Section One: Pushing the Edge of Thought

1. Robert Kaplan, "What to Ask the Person in the Mirror," *Harvard Business Review* (January 2007).

2. Tom Kelley and David Kelley, "Reclaim Your Creative Confidence—How to get over the fears that block your best ideas," *Harvard Business Review* (December 2012).

3. Marshall McLuhan and Quentin Fiore, *The Medium is the Massage: An Inventory of Effects* (Bantam Books, 1967). Note: When the book came back from the typesetter's, it had on the cover "Massage" as it still does. The title was supposed to have read "The Medium is the Message" but the typesetter had made an error. When Marshall saw the typo, he exclaimed, "Leave it alone! It's great, and right on target!"

4. Reference readings include:

Dianne Schilling, "10 Steps to Effective Listening," *Forbes.com,* November 9, 2012, https://www.forbes.com/sites/womensme-dia/2012/11/09/10-steps-to-effective-listening/#54b430803891.

John W. Link and Jo Lee Loveland Link, "10 Steps to Active Listening: A Toolset for Communications," *LinkedIn.com,* August 31, 2015, https://www.linkedin.com/pulse/10-steps-active-listening-toolset-workplace-john-link.

Jack Zenger and Joseph Folkman, "What Great Listeners Actually Do," *Harvard Business Review* (blog), July 14, 2016, https://hbr.org/2016/07/what-great-listeners-actually-do.

Emma Seppala and Jennifer Stevenson, "In a Difficult Conversation, Listen More Than You Talk," *Harvard Business Review* (blog), February 9, 2017, https://hbr.org/2017/02/in-a-difficult-conversation-listen-more-than-you-talk.

5. Manfred F. R. Kets de Vries, "Are You Too Afraid to Succeed?" *Harvard Business Review* (blog), March 4, 2014, https://hbr.org/2014/03/are-you-too-afraid-to-succeed.

6. Jarod Kintz, *This Book is NOT FOR SALE* (Amazon Digital Services LLC., 2011), Kindle Edition.

7. Amit Bhattacharjee and Cassie Mogilner, "Happiness from Ordinary and Extraordinary Experiences," *Journal of Consumer Research* 41, no. 1 (2014): 1–17.

Section Two: Pushing the Edge of Possibility

8. Steve Pavlina, "How to Discover Your Life Purpose in About 20 Minutes," *StevePavlina.com*, January 16, 2005, https://www.stevepavlina.com/blog/2005/01/how-to-discover-your-life-purpose-in-about-20-minutes/.

9. Amy Martinez, "4 Steps to Boost Your Personal Energy Reserves," *U.S. News & World Report* (blog), May 23, 2012, http://money.usnews.com/money/blogs/outside-voices-careers/2012/05/23/4-steps-to-boost-your-personal-energy-reserves-.

10. James Truslow Adams, *The Epic of America* (Oxford University Press, 1931).

11. Robert Fulghum, *All I Really Need to Know I Learned in Kindergarten: Uncommon Thoughts on Common Things* (Random House Publishing Group, 1986).

12. Senthamizh Selvan, ResearchGate (blog), September 16, 2011. https://www.researchgate.net/post/It_is_better_to_be_roughly_right_than_precisely_wrong_John_Maynard_Keynes

13. Simon Sinek, "How great leaders inspire action," TEDx Puget Sound Talk, September 2009, https://www.ted.com/talks/simon_sinek_how_great_leaders_inspire_action.

14. Simon Sinek, "How great leaders inspire action."

Section Three: Pushing the Edge of Action

15. Debra Fine, "What to Say When You Don't Know What to Say," *Huffington Post*, February 19, 2015, http://www.huffingtonpost.com/debra-fine/what-to-say-when-you-dont_1_b_6709694.html.

16. Henrik Edberg, "How to Overcome the I Don't Know What to Say Syndrome," *The Positivity Blog*, http://www.positivityblog.com/how-to-overcome-the-i-dont-know-what-to-say-syndrome/.

17. Wikiquote contributors, "Alan Kay," *Wikiquote*, accessed April 5, 2017, https://en.wikiquote.org/w/index.php?title=Alan_Kay&oldid=2189998.

18. Gail Sheehy, *Passages: Predictable Crises of Adult Life* (Ballantine Books, 1974).

19. Daniel Levinson, *The Seasons of a Man's Life* (Ballantine Books, 1978).

20. Maurice Schweitzer, "I'm Sorry: Now Was That So Hard?" *Knowledge@Wharton* (blog), University of Pennsylvania, May 23, 2011, http://knowledge.wharton.upenn.edu/article/im-sorry-now-was-that-so-hard/.

21. *Merriam-Webster Dictionary*, s.v. "melting pot," accessed April 5, 2017, https://www.merriam-webster.com/dictionary/melting%20pot.

22. *Merriam-Webster Dictionary*, s.v. "pluralism," accessed April 5, 2017, https://www.merriam-webster.com/dictionary/pluralism.

23. Wikipedia contributors, "Think different," *Wikipedia*, The Free Encyclopedia, accessed April 5, 2017, https://en.wikipedia.org/w/index.php?title=Think_different&oldid=771905294.

24. "Here's to the Crazy Ones" was the first television ad created for Apple's "Think Different" campaign, 1997, https://www.youtube.com/watch?v=QjvrBzYt3d8.

25. Albert Mehrabian, *Silent Messages: Implicit Communication of Emotions and Attitudes,* 2nd ed. (Wadsworth, 1981).

26. Malcolm Gladwell, *David and Goliath: Underdogs, Misfits, and the Art of Battling Giants* (Little Brown, 2008).

27. Robert Feldman, *The Liar in Your Life: The Way to Truthful Relationships* (Twelve, 2009).

28. Manfred F. R. Kets de Vries, "The Eight Archetypes of Leadership," *Harvard Business Review* (blog), December 18, 2013, https://hbr.org/2013/12/the-eight-archetypes-of-leadership.

About Glenn Mangurian

Glenn Mangurian is a business leader with more than four decades of experience driving innovation and results with his clients. Through personal experience, he has discovered that we are capable of overcoming challenges that seem insurmountable.

As a former senior vice president with CSC Index, Glenn was responsible for commercializing the concept of business reengineering. During his earlier professional career, he experienced many growth challenges, including geographic expansion, market reinvention, and acquisition.

In May 2001, Glenn suffered an injury to his spinal cord, resulting in the paralysis of his lower body. Undeterred by his injury, Glenn remains active in his consulting, speaking, and writing. He combines his decades of business experience with his personal experience in overcoming adversity to inspire individuals and organizations to achieve extraordinary results. He has published several articles on change management, business reengineering, and resilience. Drawing on his personal experience, he authored an article titled "Realizing What You're Made Of," which was published in March 2007 in the *Harvard Business Review*. He is a frequent speaker on the subjects of leadership and resilience. Glenn also teaches a leadership course for the University of Massachusetts. Recently he served as Chair of the Court Management Advisory Board to the Massachusetts judicial system.

Glenn has an undergraduate degree in mathematics and an MBA from University of Massachusetts Amherst. In 2003 he was awarded the Distinguished Alumni Award.

He remains active with his career, family, and community. Glenn resides with his wife, Gail, in Hingham, Massachusetts. They have two adult children and two grandchildren.

You can contact Glenn at glenn@glennmangurian.com. He welcomes your comments.

Made in the USA
Middletown, DE
17 November 2018